Advance Praise for
The Difficult Sayings of Jesus

William P. Tuck's new book [gives readers] and preachers to rejoice, because they know they can invariably count on Bill's writings to be fresh, reliable, and appealing. *The Difficult Sayings of Jesus* will be especially welcome, for it casts new light on some of the most important concepts in biblical faith and reminds us of how eminently preachable and exciting those concepts can be.

—*John Killinger*
Author of 101 Tips for New Ministers *and*
101 Tips for Minister's Spouses

William Powell Tuck finds precious wisdom lying just beneath the surface of fifteen difficult sayings of Jesus. Tuck addresses the difficulties head-on, and he tells dozens of down-to-earth stories that convey the realistic wisdom of Jesus into our world today. The result is a warm-hearted, clear-headed book in which the challenge of Jesus is felt deeply and the gospel is affirmed joyously. The chapters on prayer and on the law are brilliant, and the final chapter on hope is, well, full of hope.

—*Fisher Humphreys*
Professor of Divinity, Emeritus, Samford University

Any serious student of the New Testament, laity or clergy, raises questions about some of the teachings of Jesus. Is the resurrection believable? Why should I pray to an all-knowing God? How do you deal with passages where Jesus contradicts himself? There are also issues just begging for explanation. What is the unpardonable sin? What is Jesus' teaching on divorce? This book is a masterful guide for the minister seeking to preach on difficult texts in the Gospels. This book is also a very accessible and readable guide for the laity as they seek to understand the troubling teachings of Jesus. Tuck blends his scholarship with an ease of understanding that communicates well to a wide audience of believers and unbelievers alike.

—*Thomas Graves*
President Emeritus, Baptist Theological Seminary at Richmond

While all Christians would acknowledge the importance of Jesus' teachings, if we are honest with ourselves, few of us give every teaching the same weight. Some are simply too hard to bear and others too challenging to understand, or so we think. It may well be that the more trying sayings of Jesus are the ones we most need to hear because of how they allow God's truth to soften the hardest places in our souls. In *The Difficult Sayings of Jesus*, Bill Tuck expounds on some of these teachings and shows us how they can strengthen our devotion and give credibility to our witness, particularly in a day when many would characterize such sayings as irrelevant or unrealistic. This book is neither for the faint-hearted nor the faint-minded. But for those who desire a "red-letter" life, it will be more than worth the effort as Tuck's treatment of these difficult teachings reclaims sayings we may have ignored for too long, the very ones which despite their complexity hold the most promise for our spiritual growth.

—*Doug Dortch*
Pastor, Mountain Brook Baptist Church
Birmingham, Alabama

Every Christian has the experience of reading along in the Gospels and coming to a saying of Jesus that brings a person up short. Sometimes we puzzle over the clarity of the verse. Sometimes we puzzle over the meaning. Sometimes, a saying seems to have a hard edge that is out of character for how we think of Jesus. Noted preacher and scholar of preaching, William Powell Tuck, looks at 15 such sermons ranging from whether Jesus was serious about cutting off a hand that offends you through Jesus' seemingly intractable teaching on divorce to what Jesus might mean by eating Jesus' flesh and drinking his blood. In each case, Tuck is exegetically careful to place the text in its historical and literary context so as to identify what the text really means. He is astute in thinking about the theological claims of the text. And he is hermeneutically pastoral in finding illuminating, practical, and compassionate interpretations. The sermons are lively. They move well. And the stories are worth the price of the book. Preachers and other readers will discover that if they face into these hard sayings in the company of wise guide William Powell Tuck, they will come away ever more impressed with the wisdom of Jesus.

—*Ronald J. Allen*
Professor of Preaching, and Gospels and Letters
Christian Theological Seminary

A pastoral treasure, rich and full of insight based on years of pastoral experience and meditation on scriptures, *The Difficult Sayings of Jesus* could serve as a valuable handbook for ministers or serious students of Christian faith and would enrich and enliven classes in Christian spirituality, retreats, or personal meditation.

—E. Glenn Hinson
Emeritus Professor, Spirituality and Church History
Baptist Theological Seminary at Richmond

Smyth & Helwys Publishing, Inc.
6316 Peake Road
Macon, Georgia 31210-3960
1-800-747-3016
©2018 by William Powell Tuck
All rights reserved.

Library of Congress Cataloging-in-Publication Data

Names: Tuck, William Powell, 1934- author.
Title: The difficult sayings of Jesus / by William Powell Tuck.
Description: Macon : Smyth & Helwys, 2018.
Identifiers: LCCN 2018005139 | ISBN 9781641730181 (pbk. : alk. paper)
Subjects: LCSH: Jesus Christ--Words.
Classification: LCC BT306 .T83 2018 | DDC 232.9/54--dc23
LC record available at https://lccn.loc.gov/2018005139

Disclaimer of Liability: With respect to statements of opinion or fact available in this work of nonfiction, Smyth & Helwys Publishing Inc. nor any of its employees, makes any warranty, express or implied, or assumes any legal liability or responsibility for the accuracy or completeness of any information disclosed, or represents that its use would not infringe privately-owned rights.

THE **DIFFICULT SAYINGS OF JESUS**

WILLIAM POWELL TUCK

Also by William Powell Tuck

The Way for All Seasons
Facing Grief and Death
The Struggle for Meaning (editor)
Knowing God: Religious Knowledge in the Theology of John Baillie
Our Baptist Tradition
Ministry: An Ecumenical Challenge (editor)
Getting Past the Pain
A Glorious Vision
The Bible as Our Guide for Spiritual Growth (editor)
Authentic Evangelism
The Lord's Prayer Today
Through the Eyes of a Child
Christmas Is for the Young . . . Whatever Their Age
Love as a Way of Living
The Compelling Faces of Jesus
The Left Behind Fantasy
The Ten Commandments: Their Meaning Today
Facing Life's Ups and Downs
The Church in Today's World
The Church Under the Cross
Modern Shapers of Baptist Thought in America
The Journey to the Undiscovered Country: What's Beyond Death?
A Pastor Preaching: Toward a Theology of the Proclaimed Word
The Pulpit Ministry of the Pastors of River Road Church, Baptist (editor)
The Last Words from the Cross
Lord, I Keep Getting a Busy Signal: Reaching for a Better Spiritual Connection
Overcoming Sermon Block: The Preacher's Workshop
The Last Words from the Cross
A Revolutionary Gospel: Salvation in the Theology of Walter Rauschenbusch
Holidays, Holy Days, and Special Days
A Positive Word for Christian Lamenting: Funeral Homilies
The Forgotten Beatitude: Worshiping through Stewardship
Star Thrower: A Pastor's Handbook
A Pastoral Prophet: Sermons and Prayers of Wayne E. Oates (editor)
The Abiding Presence: Communion Meditations
Which Voice Will You Follow?

For my grandchildren

J. T., Michael, Emily, Campbell, and Alden

*May you find answers in the teachings of Jesus
to offer guidance along life's pathway.*

Author's Note

Some Scripture quotations are from the New Revised Standard Version of the Bible (NRSV), copyright © 1989 by the Division of the Christian Education of the National Council of the Churches of Christ in the USA.
Scripture quotations marked NEB or New English Bible are taken from the New English Bible, copyright © Cambridge University Press and Oxford University Press 1961, 1970.
All rights reserved.
Some Scriptures are the author's translations.

Contents

Preface	xi
1. The Unpardonable Sin (Mark 3:28-29)	1
2. What Does Eating Jesus' Flesh and Drinking His Blood Really Mean? (John 6:53-56)	11
3. Turning the Other Cheek (Matt 5:38-42)	17
4. How Can I Keep from Judging Others? (Matt 7:1-5)	27
5. The Danger of Anger (Matt 5:21-24)	37
6. How Can I Love My Enemies? (Matt 5:43-44)	45
7. When It's Hard to Forgive (Matt 18:21-35)	51
8. If God Already Knows, Why Should I Pray? (Matt 6:5-8)	59
9. Jesus' Teaching on Divorce (Matt 5:31-32; Mark 10:1-12)	71
10. When Jesus Doesn't Bring Peace (Matt 10:34-39; 12:46-50)	83
11. The Hand that Offends You (Matt 5:29-30)	91
12. Is It Possible to Live by the Golden Rule? (Matt 7:12)	99
13. Who Can Be Perfect? (Matt 5:47-48)	109
14. The Jot and Tittle of Religion (Matt 5:17-21)	119
15. How Can Jesus Be the Resurrection and the Life? (John 11:17-44)	127

Preface

Many find much comfort and assurance in thinking of Jesus as the Good Shepherd, our friend, comforter, and guide. His words like "My peace I leave with you" (John 14:27), "I do not call you servants but friends" (John 15:15), "As the Father has loved me, so I have loved you" (John 15:9), "Ask and it will be given you; search, and you will find; knock, and the door will be opened for you" (Matt 7:7), and many others offer us hope and reassurance. But other sayings of Jesus often challenge and disturb our thinking and leave us uncertain how to understand, apply, or discern the meaning intended by Jesus. Some of his more difficult sayings have been used by the enemies of Christianity to throw derision and ridicule on his teachings.

Some scholars have suggested that there might be seventy or as many as one hundred and fifty difficult teachings of Jesus. Some believe that many of Jesus' teachings are especially hard to comprehend clearly in today's world. F. F. Bruce lists seventy in his book *The Hard Sayings of Jesus* while William Neil lists sixty-five in his books *The Difficult Sayings of Jesus* and *More Difficult Sayings of Jesus*. More recent studies have been done by Richard John Neuhaus, Michael Kelly, David Bivin and Roy Blizzard Jr., Ron Rhodes, John and James Carroll, Lloyd Ogilvie, Joel Seifert, R. C. Sproul, and others. These writers note the difficulty in translating the words of Jesus from Aramaic or Hebrew. They believe that much of the difficulty may lie in Jesus' use of simile, metaphors, puns, hyperbole, overstatements, irony, paradox, proverbs, riddles, poetic forms, and parallelism.

The difficult sayings I am referring to are evident in the following: "Whoever does not hate father and mother cannot be my disciple" (Luke 14:26ff.), "You must be perfect as your heavenly father is perfect" (Matt 5:48), "Love your enemies" (Matt 5:44), "If your right eye causes you to sin, pluck it out" (Matt 5:29), "Go sell what you have" (Mark 10:21), and "Unless you eat the flesh of the Son of Man and drink his blood . . ." (John 6:53). To try to ignore the difficulty of these teachings or simply to act like they are not puzzling is dishonest. As Christians, we need to attempt to grasp their intended message—especially if we expect to preach or teach about them. Sometimes we have to acknowledge that some of the perplexing teachings of Jesus may be clear enough, but trying to apply them to our own situation may be more complicated than we thought. At other times, the teaching may be clear, like the command against divorce, but we lack the will or moral determination to follow it.

On other occasions, the hard sayings may challenge our apathy, indecision, callousness about holy things, or commitment to genuinely following Jesus. Other hard teachings remind us of the difficulty and challenge of walking in the Christ-like way. Still others probe deeply into our souls to enlist us to reach for the highest and best within us as followers of the "narrow" way. These teachings may become instruments to enable us to grow spiritually and discern what it means to "take up our cross and follow" Christ.

The "hard sayings" raise many difficult questions for us. But questions arise about God's presence or practice in other issues, like the suffering and death of loved ones and the devastation that occurs in war, hurricanes, floods, earthquakes, or other natural disasters. Many of our questions scream, "Why? Where is God?" Many of the psalms are filled with such laments, like Psalms 5, 6, 13, 22, 38, 51, 103, 130, and others. Listen to the writer of Psalm 102: "Hear my prayer, O LORD; let my cry come to you. Do not hide your face from me in the day of my distress." I do not believe that it is wrong or sinful to ask questions of God or to express fear, worries, or concerns to God. Elie Wiesel indicated that all his life he had been content to ask questions about God and his creation knowing that "the questions are eternal; the answers never are." But he learned that God "is to be found in the questions as well as in the answers." Nevertheless, even with all his questions, he affirmed, "I confess to having rebelled against the Lord, but I have never repudiated Him."[1] It's okay to raise questions to God. We may not have all the answers to our questions, but we know the Answerer.

So we can look honestly at the difficult sayings of Jesus and the questions they may raise without avoiding or denying their difficulty. We can seek to examine them without fear that our inquiries are wrong or unchristian, knowing that God understands our desire for clarity. I believe that a preacher or teacher should not try to "explain away" the difficult and, at times, the shocking demand that Jesus presents in these teachings. Without question, they cut against the grain of our modern world and our comfortable way of trying to make the teachings of Jesus acceptable and attractive to people. These hard words represent the challenges and expectations Jesus has for those who would follow him. We need to interpret them and understand them but not lessen their demands. The following fifteen selections are one minister's attempt to wrestle with some of the difficult sayings of Jesus.[2]

I want to express my appreciation to my good friend and fellow minister, Rand Forder, for his thorough proofreading of my manuscript.

Notes

1. Elie Wiesel, *Open Heart* (New York: Schocken Books, 2012) 68–69.

2. In chapter 6 of my book, *Lord, I Keep Getting a Busy Signal*—titled "When You Can't Pray Anymore"—I treat another difficult saying of Jesus in his response to a woman in Tyre and Sidon, Gentile territory, who begged for her child to be healed (Matt 15:21-28). See William Powell Tuck, *Lord, I Keep Getting a Busy Signal: Reaching for a Better Spiritual Connection* (Gonzalez FL: Energion Publications, 2014) 85–96.

1

The Unpardonable Sin

Mark 3:28-29

Some time ago I visited a woman in the hospital who was dying. She, like most people facing death, had many fears. One of the reasons for her fears, which she acknowledged to me, was that she thought she had committed the unpardonable sin. She was afraid that when she died she would not be allowed in the presence of God and could not go to heaven because of this sin. Through extended conversation with her, I discovered that what she called her "unpardonable sin" was some sexual activity in which she had engaged earlier in her life and for which she had not found forgiveness.

I have talked with several people who were afraid they had committed the unpardonable sin. They had not experienced forgiveness for something wrong that they had done in the past. Their prayers seemed to go unanswered, and God seemed remote, distant, and unresponsive. Some of them expressed a great deal of anger toward God. Many pastoral counselors, psychologists, and psychiatrists have talked with such people. But counselors have discovered that other problems often lie behind this anguish. Behind the fear of having committed the unpardonable sin was unresolved guilt for some sexual activity at an earlier stage of life or unresolved grief over the death of a loved one—a husband or wife, parent, or child. The fear of having committed the unpardonable sin may veil fears about a child to be born, aging, the loss of a job, a sudden illness, or many other factors. Such people need professional help to come to grips with their continuing struggle with the "unpardonable" sin. Their fear may be a mask to disguise a deeper problem.

A Disturbing Word

I have discovered that people think Jesus' words about a sin that is unpardonable are startling, especially coming from Jesus. Listen to the words again: "Truly I tell you, people will be forgiven for their sins and whatever blasphemies they utter; but whoever blasphemes against the Holy Spirit can never have forgiveness, but is guilty of an eternal sin" (Mark 3:28-29, NRSV). These words have caused misery, discomfort, terror, and anguish for people because they are afraid that they somehow committed this unpardonable sin. They are afraid that they will be shut out of the presence of God when they die and cannot experience forgiveness in this life. Let's be honest and say at the beginning that this *is* a rather startling word from Jesus. Halford Luccock expressed this feeling:

> If with reverence, a list of the sayings of Jesus could be assembled under the heading, "Things I wish Jesus had never said." . . . This word on the "unforgivable sin" has had a strange fascination and terror for many minds. The distorting of it has filled insane asylums with minds broken down by a guilt complex . . . . Yet the context makes the meaning clear and simple.[1]

We are startled by these words of Jesus that there can be an unforgivable sin because the heart of the gospel is forgiveness. Our Lord declared, "Whosoever will may come unto me." We learned to quote as children the words of John 3:16, "For God so loved the world that he gave his only begotten son that whosoever believes in him should not perish." Jesus taught about God's love through parables about a lost son, a lost sheep, and a lost coin; all of them symbolize our acceptance by God. The psalmist wrote that the wideness of God's forgiveness removes our sins as far as the east is from the west. Even the dying thief's prayer on the cross that Jesus remember him received this generous response from Jesus: "This day you will be with me in Paradise." So we have to be honest and say that these words in Mark 3:28-29 are upsetting. They seem to contradict God's unconditional love.

The Biblical Context

To try to get an answer, let's begin by noticing the setting of this story. Whenever we examine a text, we need to consider its context. Too often we select a Scripture passage but do not take account of the setting in which that passage occurred. The setting for these harsh words from Jesus is in

Galilee right after he healed a man who had been possessed by demons. Some of the Pharisees and scribes came down from Jerusalem into Galilee where Jesus was teaching and healing and accused Jesus of healing not by the power of God's Spirit but by the power of Beelzebub. Beelzebub was an old Canaanite word that meant "the prince of demons." The Pharisees accused Jesus of doing his good works by the power of the chief of demons—Satan.

An Emphatic Response

Notice the emphatic response of Jesus to the Pharisees. This phrase has been translated in various ways: "Verily I say unto you . . ." or "Truly I say unto you . . ." or "I tell you this . . . ." This phrase is sometimes translated "amen." Jesus himself is described in Revelation as "the Amen"—the faithful witness. Jesus was saying, "What I'm saying to you now is extremely important, and you need to listen carefully." Jesus begins by confronting the Pharisees with the absurdity of claiming that Satan is behind the good things Jesus is doing. Jesus was casting out evil in people. It would not be logical to say this was the result of Satan's action. That would be like Satan trying to destroy himself. This kind of claim would be like the Allied forces intentionally dropping bombs on our own military soldiers and destroying our own forces. The Pharisees were also condemning themselves because they likewise claimed to cast out demons. They did not attribute their actions to Satan, but they attributed the good work of Jesus to the evil powers of Satan.

The Nature of the Sin Condemned

What was the nature of the sin Jesus condemned? The word used to describe this sin is called "blasphemy" in some translations and "slander" in others. The word "blaspheme" means to ridicule, to put down in a contemptuous manner, to profane or mock spiritual matters or anything regarded as sacred, to curse, to show irreverence toward God or to revile God or holy things. Jesus declared that the Pharisees were committing blasphemy because they were ascribing to Satan the good acts that Jesus was doing. They credited the powers of evil to God. They were calling good evil. Since they did not approve of Jesus or agree with his teachings, they were unwilling to acknowledge that the good he was doing came from the work of God's Spirit. Therefore, they called it evil. They were not merely maligning the character of Jesus but also slandering the nature of God. Jesus said whenever a person calls the good work of the Spirit of God evil, then that person is committing the unpardonable sin. Why? Their spiritual and moral blindness has caused them to refuse to acknowledge the obvious good that Jesus is doing and ascribe it instead to Satan. They have gotten to the point in their lives where they are totally oblivious to their own blindness and the nature of their sin. This can happen to anyone.

Let's take an example. With the continuing wars in Iraq, especially with ISIS and other rebels, there will likely be ongoing food shortages in that country. Suppose that many people in Baghdad, or in some other area of the country, are on the verge of starving when the ongoing conflict is finally over. The United States might decide to send in food to feed these people. After the supplies of food arrive in Baghdad or in another section of the country, suppose some of the Iraqi leaders say, "Don't eat this food. The Americans have poisoned it. Therefore, it will kill you." And the people do not eat it and starve to death. The food that is good is called evil, and because the people refuse to eat it on the advice of their leaders, they perish.

This is the kind of thing the Pharisees were saying about Jesus. He had come as the Bread of Life to feed the spirits of men and women. The One who had come to feed people and show them the way to God was being rejected by the Pharisees and accused of "poisoning" the people through the power of Satan. Blinded by their attitude toward Jesus, these Pharisees caused people to turn away from God. What was their blasphemy? It was saying that the good God was accomplishing through Jesus was evil. They reached the point where they called evil good and good evil. Their blindness made it impossible to distinguish between good and evil. Pheme Perkins believes that these words from Jesus apply primarily to the religious authorities who came from Jerusalem to investigate his teachings.[2]

Not an Isolated Act

The path to committing the unforgivable sin is a lifetime journey. The unpardonable sin is not some act that an individual commits in an isolated moment or in one single event. It is a path that a person may walk down over a long period of time. The journey on this pathway begins first in what I would call "grieving the Spirit of God." In Ephesians 4:30, Paul urges, "Do not grieve the Holy Spirit of God." God's Spirit seeks to work within our lives to strengthen us whenever temptation comes. God's Spirit whispers in our hearts to give us guidance and direction. The Holy Spirit is our advocate and helper to enable us to confront whatever difficulties lie before us. The Spirit seeks to empower us to resist temptation and not yield to its power. When we are tempted to sin, whether it is to lie, cheat, steal, or be unfaithful to a spouse, the Holy Spirit whispers gently within to guide us through this temptation. God always gives us freedom of will to decide. The choice is up to us. If we do sin, however, then we grieve God's Spirit. The first step down the path of the unpardonable sin is to grieve God's Spirit.

Resisting the Spirit

The second step is to resist the Spirit of God. The small epistle of James reminds us to "Resist the devil and he will flee from you" (Jas 4:7). Rather than resisting the powers of evil, sometimes people resist God's Spirit. Instead of following God's leadership, they turn away from God's guidance. A cartoon showed a prophet of doom dressed in a long gown as he walked down the street carrying a sign that read, "Resist Temptation." A seedy-looking guy walked up behind him, saw the sign, and said, "Personally, I'm not interested in resisting temptation. I'm trying to find some!" A church sign had the following words: "If you are tired of sin, call 896-8882." But someone wrote underneath that statement, "If not, call 715-6789."

Unfortunately, this frivolous attitude is the stance of many people toward any discussion about "sin." Our resistance to sin is not very strong. We begin to build up a resistance against the Spirit of God and slowly, ever so slowly, turn away from the Spirit's guidance. This does not happen in a moment but is a steady erosion of the influence of the good on our thinking. We don't plan to sin. But slowly, ever so slowly, we turn our back on God. We do not hear the whispers of God's Spirit as much. We begin to move away from church, cease to pray, do not come to worship, begin to ignore our church friends and God's ways. The world dominates our lives and we are insulated from God. We move down a path of resistance that carries us away from God almost without our knowing it.

Here is an example. Suppose you have a faithful friend who helps and guides you through life. You are both standing by a small stream as you walk and talk. The stream is so small that you can reach across it and touch each other. You can talk and even embrace each other across the stream because it is so narrow. As you begin to walk down one side of the stream and your friend walks down the other, you notice that the stream eventually becomes a creek, then a river, growing wider and wider. Like many streams, at certain places it twists and turns as it flows along, and there are points where you are so separated from your friend that you can no longer see each other. The force of the water has become rapid and the distance is so wide that you can't see one another and you can no longer talk or help each other. You have gradually moved away from each other. Your choice of paths separated you.

The prophet Isaiah gives this warning:

> You shall indeed hear but never understand, and you shall indeed see but never perceive. For this people's heart has grown dull, and their ears heavy of hearing, and their eyes they have closed, lest they should perceive with their eyes, and hear with their ears, and understand with their heart, and turn for me to heal them. (Isa 6:9-10)

Quenching the Spirit

Down the path to the unpardonable sin, we move from the second stage of resistance to the third level, which is to quench God's Spirit. Paul writes in 1 Thessalonians 5:19, "Quench not the Spirit of God." We quench our capacity to respond to God by pouring water on God's efforts to guide us. Our senses become unresponsive to God's efforts. We shut the door to God and close God out of our lives. Our capacity to respond to God's Spirit has gradually grown cold and dead. There is no channel open for God to work in our lives, because we have slowly turned away from him. Our hearts have become hardened; our senses are dead and our capacity to respond is muted.

Since we have not exercised our capacity to respond to God, we have lost our ability to respond. Whatever gift or sense we have in our lives, if we do not use it, we will lose it. Our bodies are certainly an example of this principle. If we do not exercise our muscles, our bodies will soon become weak and flabby. In one study, a selected group of ninety-year-old people was put through a program of exercises. They discovered that even at their advanced age, exercise with weights still improved their physical strength and vitality. Many of us lose our physical capacities simply because we do not use them. The same is true with our intellectual or musical capacities. If we don't use the gifts we have, we soon will lose them. I took both Latin and Spanish in high school, but I cannot use either language effectively today because I haven't used them through the years since then, whereas I have a better grasp of Greek and Hebrew because I have continued to use them. If you can play the piano, you must continue to practice or soon you will grow rusty. When we don't use certain capacities, they will be lost through disuse. This is also true spiritually. If we do not exercise our spiritual awareness, seek to develop our prayer lives and our spiritual depth, then this capacity will begin to shrink and will soon be lost.

Some people have already lost their sense of sin. That is Karl Menninger's disturbing message in his book, *Whatever Became of Sin?* In our society, many people no longer want to acknowledge that their wrongdoing is sin. They may acknowledge what happens as a crime or something that is the result of heredity—such as their genes or a weak trait—or the result of their environment. Some refuse to acknowledge that sin has caused them to act the way they do. What indeed has become of our sense of sin? The word "sin" seems to be disappearing from the vocabulary of our society, but, unfortunately, sin has not. Whittier expressed that truth in these lines:

> What if thine eye refuses to see,
> Thine ear of Heaven's free welcome fail,
> And thou a willing captive be,
> Thyself thy own dark jail?[3]

Losing a Sense of Sin

We can become blind to our own sin and no longer even have a sense of sin. We can lose our power to distinguish between good and bad, light and darkness. Sin is no longer a reality to us. This is what eventually happens to Dr. Jekyll in Robert Louis Stevenson's tale of *Dr. Jekyll and Mr. Hyde*. After a while, the darker side of Mr. Hyde begins to dominate until the good side of Dr. Jekyll is silenced. Dr. Jekyll begins to realize what is happening to him and he declares,

> The balance of my nature might be permanently overthrown, the power of voluntary change be forfeited and the character of Edward Hyde becomes irrevocably mine. . . . I was slowly losing hold of my original and better self, and becoming slowly incorporated with my second and worst.[4]

Our sinful self can take over the control of our life and we can lose our sense of sin. But an even sadder fact is that we can get to a point where we, like the Pharisees in this text, call good evil and evil good. The witches in Shakespeare's *Macbeth* were at this place. They cried, "Foul is fair and fair is foul."[5] Some reach the point where they no longer are able to distinguish good and evil. Milton's Satan is there when he cries, "Evil be thou my good."[6] These people are amoral. Their concept of right and wrong is so confused that they can no longer distinguish good from evil.

The Mammoth Caves in Virginia contain fish that are able to swim in the darkest regions. These fish are blind. Even if they were brought to a bright, sparkling lake under the sun, they would still be blind. An examination of the fish's eyes shows that they appear normal. But studies have proven that the optic nerves in their eyes have shriveled from disuse and cannot respond to light. If an individual lives in darkness for too long, he or she can get beyond the point of responding to the grace of God.

Remorse Makes It Unlikely

Now hear this word of comfort: if you think you have committed the unpardonable sin, that is a sure sign that you haven't. Your very concern over your sin indicates that you have not closed yourself to God's Spirit. Your remorse indicates that you are still trying to understand God's ways and be responsive to God. Most people who worry about committing the unpardonable sin are not those who have actually done it. Paul Tournier, in his book *Guilt and Grace*, makes this point clear.

> But in truth, this saying of Christ is not addressed to anyone in distress . . . who is afraid of blaspheming, and who may for that very reason give way to a blasphemous thought; but on the contrary, it is for someone full of self-satisfaction and with no conviction of guilt who scorns salvation and the gift of the Holy Spirit. So we may say with certainty that anyone who is worried with having committed the sin against the Holy Spirit has not committed it, precisely because he or she is worried.[7]

Hardened to Our Sins

There is a warning in these words from Jesus that we all need to hear. There is the possibility that we can become so hardened in our sin that we are not able to see God's good works in the lives of others. Because of our modern understanding of the Trinity, many may not understand how Jesus could make a distinction between his work and the work of the Holy Spirit. Jesus in his wisdom knew that people might misunderstand and reject him. Even his disciples misunderstood his teachings and could not comprehend that he had to die on a cross. If people rejected Jesus' human witness, that could be forgiven. But what could not be forgiven was for people to witness the good works God was doing through the Son by the power of the Holy Spirit and call that good evil.

The preacher C. G. Holt was delivering a sermon in a church in England on this very passage several years ago. In the course of his sermon, he looked down and saw a beautiful bouquet of flowers on the table in front of the pulpit. "There are bad men in this district," he said, "but I do not think there is one so depraved as to say that the growth, the beauty, and the fragrance of these flowers are the work of the devil. In the lower sense that would be sinning against the Holy Ghost." Later he received a letter from the daughter of the gardener in the church, who thought he had committed the unpardonable sin. But she said that day, her father, the gardener, realized he had not. "Bad as I have been," the gardener said, as he stood before a rose bush in full bloom, "I have never said that these flowers were the creation of the devil. No, my Father made them all."

So hear the good news in this biblical text. Hear the part of this Scripture where Jesus says, "I tell you no sin, no slander is beyond forgiveness." Acknowledge that great truth. The slander against the Holy Spirit may never be forgiven. But remember that no sin or slander is beyond God's forgiveness as long as you and I are willing to confess those sins. The problem does not lie with God's unwillingness to pardon us. The problem lies with one who is unwilling to acknowledge that he or she has sinned and is unwilling to confess that sin. This is the truth that is stated in the small epistle of First John. The writer says,

> If we say that we have no sin, we deceive ourselves and the truth is not in us. If we confess our sins, he is faithful and just to forgive us our sins and to cleanse us from all unrighteousness. If we say that we have not sinned, we make him a liar and his word is not in us. (1 John 1:6-10)

The One Unforgivable Sin

The only sin God cannot forgive is the sin that a person is unwilling to confess or acknowledge. God is always willing to forgive. So unlock your heart, and don't worry about having committed the unpardonable sin. If you are concerned at all about your sins, be assured that God will forgive you. As Jesus said, "Whosoever will may come."

Joseph Fort Newton told about a man who was in deep misery in his soul. As he walked down a country lane in the back regions of England, he wandered until he was exhausted and sat by a hedge to rest. While he was resting he overheard two young women on the other side of the hedge talking about a sermon one of them had heard by a preacher in a London church. "I heard him preach once and I shall never forget one thing that he said. It gave me a big lift." "Oh, really!" the other woman said. "What did he say?" Her friend responded, "The world will always say, 'You have made your bed and you must lie in it'; but One greater than the world has said,

'Take up your bed and walk. Your sins are forgiven.'" The despairing man, upon hearing that word, found a burden lifted from his life.

The world says, "You have made your bed. Tough stuff!" But God's good news to us is, "You can be forgiven no matter what your sin is." Confess and repent of your sins. God's grace is abundant. His love is unconditional. If you think you have committed the unpardonable sin, quit worrying. You haven't. Accept God's grace and forgiveness. God wants to love you. Accept God's grace and follow God.

Notes

1. Halford Luccock, "The Gospel According to St. Mark," *The Interpreter's Bible* (Nashville: Abingdon-Cokesbury Press, 1951) 693.

2. Pheme Perkins, "The Gospel of Mark," *The New Interpreter's Bible* (Nashville: Abingdon Press, 1995) 564.

3. John Greenleaf Whittier, "The Answer," stanza XV.

4. Robert Louis Stevenson, *The Complete Short Stories of Robert Louis Stevenson*, ed. Charles Neider (Garden City NY: Doubleday, 1969) 528.

5. William Shakespeare, *Macbeth*, act I, scene I.

6. Quoted in Luccock, "The Gospel According to St. Mark."

7. Paul Tournier, *Guilt and Grace* (New York: Harper & Row, 1962) 153.

2

What Does Eating Jesus' Flesh and Drinking His Blood Really Mean?

John 6:53-56

Several years ago, I stayed up most of the night reading a true story written by Piers Paul Read titled *Alive: The Story of the Andes Survivors.* A plane carrying forty-five people, most of whom had been in a rugby match in Santiago, crashed into the mountains in the Andes. Of the forty-five people on the plane, twenty-seven were still alive following the plane crash. When the plane fell into the freezing snow, it broke in half. The people had little clothing, and what they had was very light since they had been in a warm climate before. Among those who survived was a young man who had a steel rod sticking through his stomach. Others had broken bones and internal injuries.

Only sixteen of the twenty-seven made it off the mountain. They survived basically by caring for each other. Those people, like the young man with the steel rod stuck in his body, assisted others who were hurt worse than they were. Those who were strong attempted to help the weaker ones. They had almost no food except for a few dates, some crackers, a little jelly, a few candy bars, and a bit of wine. They rationed the food to each other by breaking the crackers, the candy, and other items into tiny bites.

They had no utensils, so they drank the wine from a deodorant can top. In a few days, the food was gone. But they survived for seventy-one days.

One of the young men who was there wrote these words:

> It was something that no one could have imagined. I used to go to mass every Sunday, and Holy Communion had become something automatic. [All of the crash victims were Catholic.] But up there, seeing so many miracles, being so near God, almost touching him, I learned otherwise. Now I pray to God to give me strength and stop me slipping back to what I used to be. I have learned that life is love, and that love is giving to your neighbor . . . . There is nothing better than giving to a fellow human being.[1]

Remember, they had such a small amount to give, yet in that crisis, they learned a powerful lesson: that the ultimate meaning in life is found in loving your fellow human being.

But that is not the entire story. They were able to survive seventy-one days because they did find a food source. They had asked, "Where shall we get food?" As they were outside the plane disposing of some of the bodies of the dead by placing them in the snow, one of them said to another, "I know that if my dead body could help you to stay alive, then I'd certainly want you to use it."[2] They made a pact then that if others died, they would use their bodies for food.

Finally, after several weeks when all the food was gone and they realized help was not going to come, they knew there was only one way they could survive. They had to have nourishment. One of them went outside and cut off some flesh from one of the bodies, then put it on one of the plane wings to allow it to dry enough to eat. He then swallowed it and reflected, "It's like Holy Communion. When Christ died he gave his body to us so that we could have spiritual life. My friend has given us his body so that we can have physical life."[3] They survived because they literally fed off those who had already given their lives. Several of them finally got strong enough from eating this meat that they were able to climb over the mountain and reach help for the others. In their first interview after they were rescued, they shared this fact with people, and many were shocked. But the local priest did not condemn them and neither did most of the newspapers. For them, the act in which they had participated became a spiritual experience.

Eating Jesus' Flesh and Drinking His Blood

When Jesus told his followers, "You are to eat my flesh and drink my blood," was he telling them to be cannibalistic? If you read further in this biblical passage, you will discover in the sixtieth verse that when the people heard this teaching from Jesus, they replied, "This is a hard saying." Some scholars have translated the Greek to read, "This is more than we can stomach! Why listen to such talk?" (NEB 6:60). This saying was so offensive that some of Jesus' disciples turned and walked away and would no longer follow him. They could not imagine a Jew eating flesh and drinking blood! There were laws that condemned such action (Gen 9:4; Deut 16:23). To the Jewish person, blood represented life. Jews would drain every drop of blood from any carcass before they would eat it. The thought of drinking the blood and eating the flesh of Jesus was offensive to them!

The Jewish leaders had asked Jesus earlier, "Are you greater than Moses? Moses gave Israel bread in the wilderness. Can you equal that?" Moses had been the means God used to lead the people through the wilderness. Jesus had just fed five thousand people in the wilderness place. Jesus was declaring that he was greater than Moses. And he was. Jesus was not simply the giver of the bread; he was and is the Bread. Jesus was telling them, "*I am your source of life!*"

A Deep Mystery

This is still a hard saying for us today, isn't it? We don't like it much either. It is still offensive, if we think about it. Let's see if we can understand what Jesus meant. I want to offer three brief suggestions. First, whenever we seek to understand our spiritual fellowship with God, we are aware of a deep mystery. Who can really explain what it means to be in Christ or for Christ to be in us? I grow weary with people who want to put this mystery in such simple language. They do harm to our faith by wanting everything to be simplistic. At the heart of our religion lies the greatest mystery in the world. The mystery of how we receive God's grace and how we relate to God evades simple words or even profound theological thought. The symbolism of the bread and the cup at the Lord's Table acknowledges this mystery again. Our relationship to God cannot be defined in words. Words fall short and are always theologically inadequate. That's the reason we seek to display our Lord's sacrifice symbolically through the bread and the cup. These pictures or images tell us more than words can convey.

The world in which Jesus gave these instructions was filled with all kinds of religious traditions, including the mystery religions. In some of the ancient religions around Israel, adherents would prepare meat and offer it to be sacrificed to their god. All of the meat would not be sacrificed, but the people would eat some of the meat that had been a part of the sacrifice. They thought that by eating this meat, the flesh offered to their god, they were literally taking the god into their bodies. Paul wrote about this problem in the Corinthian church. The Corinthian Christians struggled with the question, "Should we eat meat that has been offered to idols?" Jesus knew what the people thought about such matters, and he drew on this notion that the people commonly held.

Incorporating Christ into Our Lives

Second, I think Jesus' saying about eating his flesh and drinking his blood basically means that we have to assimilate, receive, or incorporate Jesus Christ, the Word who was made flesh, into our lives. John was writing to some who wanted to deny the humanity of Jesus. John stressed the humanity of Jesus in his declaration, "The Word became flesh." Every believer has to acknowledge Jesus' humanity and affirm the Incarnation and receive him by faith. When we eat physical food, it enters into our bodies and is assimilated and digested so it is absorbed into our systems and we are nourished by it. Our food becomes a part of us. Faith is to our spirits what food is to our bodies. Jesus instructs us about the necessity of feeding on him. We receive him as bread for our spiritual bodies and are nourished by him as we incorporate his presence into our inner being. Alan Culpepper notes that the metaphorical language of eating and drinking has Eucharistic overtones and refers to receiving Jesus and the life he offers.[4]

Unless you and I receive Christ, we really can't "feed" on him. I have many fine theological books in my library. I have a marvelous book by Jurgen Moltmann, the German theologian, titled *The Crucified God*. If that book just sits on my shelf and I never read it, it doesn't help me to grow spiritually. I have to be willing to take it off the shelf, open it, and read it. In reading it, I learn something from it and am "fed" by it. We have a beautiful recording of Handel's *Messiah* at our house. The recording can sit on the shelf forever, but I can't enjoy it or be enriched by it unless I am willing to play it. When I am exposed to it, it penetrates my mind and heart. The Gospel of John has many marvelous truths and stories about the life and ministry of Jesus, but unless you and I are willing to read them and receive them, this Gospel doesn't influence us.

I believe that Jesus is using a metaphor in our text that is similar to one we use today. We sometimes say that a person "devours" certain things.

Some people devour books; others devour music. Another person may "drink in" a concert. Or lovers are "drinking each other in." On other occasions, we declare, "I can't stomach that!" That's another way of saying, "I don't like it." Others sometimes say, "Let me chew on this matter for a while." Or "Don't bite off my head." We use all kinds of expressions drawn from our anatomy to express certain truths. In a similar way, Jesus used a vivid metaphor to denote the radical nature of our commitment to him. Jesus calls us to a demanding discipleship. It is not enough simply to think about him or sing about him or preach or talk about him. We have to receive him fully. Jesus has to be incorporated or assimilated into our very being. He becomes such a part of us that he transforms us. As Jesus said about his relationship to his Father, "I am in the Father and the Father is in me." Jesus wants that same kind of relationship with his disciples.

The Demanding Nature of Discipleship

Finally, how can such a demanding discipleship come about? The words about eating his flesh and drinking his blood are clear expressions of the costly nature of grace. Our salvation came about through a great sacrifice by Jesus. It cost him flesh and blood. Jesus poured out his life in love for you and me. Such sacrifice calls us to respond. To benefit from such a costly sacrifice, we have to receive it. When we receive God's love, our lives can be radically different. But we have to receive this love as we would food. As George Beasley-Murray observes, "the eating and drinking of Christ's flesh and blood result in mutual 'abiding' of the believer and Christ."[5]

The wonder of this sacrificial love is that it is for all people. *All people.* A prostitute came into a church one day and sat near the back. She noticed that they were having Communion. One of the elders approached her and extended the Communion tray to her. She hesitated. "Take it," the elder said. "It is for sinners, which we all are."

When we participate in a Communion service, we come to the Lord's Table to acknowledge God's love. We come to experience God's grace. We come as sinners all. We acknowledge that God so loved the world that God sent God's Son. But we must receive God's Son to experience this love. So, when you come to the Lord's Table, open your mouth, your ears, your eyes, your heart, your whole being, and feed on God. Thirst after God. Hunger after God. As you come to the Table, open the pores of your whole being that you might sense God's presence through the elements. I pray that each of us will truly be open and feed on God as we come to commune at the Lord's Table.

Notes

1. Piers Paul Read, *Alive: The Story of the Andes Survivors* (New York: Avon, 1974) 279–80.

2. Ibid., 77.

3. Ibid., 83.

4. R. Alan Culpepper, *The Gospel of John: Interpreting Biblical Texts* (Nashville: Abingdon Press, 1998) 163.

5. George R. Beasley-Murray, *John: Word Biblical Commentary* (Waco TX: Word Books Publishers, 1987) 95.

Turning the Other Cheek

Matthew 5:38-42

The words were shocking to me when I first read them. Maybe they will shock you too. They read like this:

> Love your enemies and do good to them that hate and use you—is this not the despicable philosophy of the spaniel that rolls upon its back when kicked? Hate your enemies with a whole heart, and if a man smites you on one cheek, smash him on the other! Smite him hip and thigh, for self-preservation is the highest law. He who turns the other cheek is a cowardly dog! Give blow for blow, scorn for scorn, doom for doom—with compound interest literally added thereunto! Make yourself a Terror to your adversary, and when he goeth his way, he will possess much additional wisdom to ruminate over. Thus shall you make yourself respected in all the walks of life, and your spirit—your immortal spirit—shall live, not in an intangible paradise, but in the brains and sinews of those whose respect you have gained.[1]

These words are from *The Satanic Bible* by Anton LaVey. Unfortunately, they reflect too much the philosophy and attitude of many of us. This philosophy, rather than Christ's teachings, has dominated people on the personal, national, and international levels. The words from Jesus that we are to love our enemies, turn the other cheek, give our second coat, or go the second mile are still as shocking, bewildering, repulsive, and revolutionary today as they were when Jesus first uttered them.

Early Concepts of Revenge

The Jewish people to whom Jesus spoke the words of Matthew 5:38-42 had experienced an evolution in their attitude toward revenge. In ancient times, if an enemy came into your village or tribe and hurt someone there or knocked your eye out in a battle or stole something of yours, you retaliated by destroying his whole village. You killed everybody you could to get your revenge. You practiced unlimited retaliation. As civilization advanced a step, the people began to practice limited retaliation. This principle was set forth in teachings like The Code of Hammurabi and Lex Talionis, which meant an eye for an eye or a tooth for a tooth. This practice was actually a step up the moral scale. If a man knocked your eye out, instead of killing him and his whole tribe, you would put out his eye. If he knocked your tooth out, rather than killing him, you would knock his tooth out. If you lost a cow, you would take a cow in return.

After a while people got to the point where they did not engage in like exchanges literally but settled for a monetary amount or paid off with animals or some form of property. Civilization then advanced to a higher level where they practiced what might be called exclusive love. A person exercised love toward friends and family but directed hatred toward enemies. The Jewish people were at this level when Jesus taught them the words of our text. Their philosophy is still in practice today. We tend to love our family and friends but hate our enemies.

Jesus' Revolutionary Teaching on Revenge

Jesus gave a new vision of resistance that was revolutionary and startling to his hearers. He taught a standard of love that had not been a part of the Jewish teachings as recorded in the Old Testament. Listen to what Jesus says: "If someone strikes you on one cheek, turn to him the other cheek." The wording implies that a person is struck again with the back of the hand. This was a double insult, but Jesus advises to turn the other cheek. Too often we lose Jesus' message by getting caught up in the literal act of someone hitting us. Jesus was dealing primarily with a person being insulted. Jesus says if someone is insulting you, then you have to be willing to accept a further insult.

Jesus uses another example. If someone asks for your tunic, which was a man's undergarment, Jesus says don't be concerned about that piece of clothing but give him your outer garment as well. A man usually had at least two tunics in ancient biblical times. But he had only one outer garment, which he often used as a blanket at night to keep him warm. To give that coat away would literally be to give up his blanket. This would have shocked Jesus' listeners. The law courts of that day said that a man might have to surrender his undergarment in a legal suit but not his outer garment. In the reference to coats, Jesus is raising a question about a person's legal right in a Jewish law court. Jesus says, "Don't be concerned about your own rights. Be concerned about helping another person."

The last example Jesus uses is about a person who lives in an occupied country and is compelled by military force to carry a soldier's pack one mile. Roman soldiers could press any Jewish citizen into being a baggage carrier. If a soldier was walking down a road and he saw you going the opposite way with your donkey, he could order you to use your donkey to carry his load or force you personally to carry his pack. Jesus says, "Don't stop at one mile. Go one more mile with him. Don't just do what the law says. You go even further than what is legally required." Simon of Cyrene was later pressed into duty to bear the cross of Jesus when Jesus fell under its load on his way to be crucified. The Roman law gave soldiers the power to press anyone they wanted to into service.

Are Jesus' Teachings on Revenge Unrealistic?

These are the basic teachings in our text from Jesus. How do people usually respond to these teachings today? Some react by saying that they are part of an idealistic, utopian, unrealistic, impractical philosophy that has nothing to do with real life. People argue that these principles would be unrealistic in the "dog-eat-dog" business world or as a means of solving the significant problems in international affairs with nations like Russia, China, Iraq, or North Korea. "How can anybody possibly live by such an absurd doctrine as this?" they ask. "If someone breaks into my home and attacks my family," they continue, "you can believe that I won't turn the other cheek. I will try to stop him. If someone has a gun and that person is aiming the gun at me, you'd better believe I will protect myself."

But this is not what Jesus means. Jesus is not asking us to be as impractical as possible. He is talking about personal relationships, not violent attacks. The reference to a slap on the face is an image of personal insult, not a possible injury. Of course you should defend yourself in such situations. Some people want to dismiss Jesus' teaching here because they try to press it too rigidly in an obvious way and refuse to see the real message behind the teaching.

Taking the Teaching Literally

There are others who take this teaching literally. The Mennonites in Holland, the Anabaptists in Germany, and the Mennonites and Quakers in the United States have taken this passage literally. Therefore, they have refused to participate in any kind of war. They have conscientiously condemned war as immoral. Many in the US who have participated in the civil rights marches and demonstrations have tried to practice these teachings literally. At times, Jesus seemed to practice what he taught here. However, his confrontation with the money changers in the temple seems to run counter to this teaching.

A Radical Call to a Higher Way

Is it possible to understand these difficult sayings of Jesus? Let me begin by saying that we need to understand that Jesus is offering his followers a radical picture of his call to a higher way of responding to personal resistance. Most of us had rather not hear the hard side of the Christian way. Jesus again and again exposed the sharp flint of his teachings. There is a sandpaper edge to his teachings that often rubs against what society wants and what we as individuals may desire for our lives. Jesus refused to water down his teachings and demands in order to get disciples. He called his followers to a higher way that demanded a radical response to the abrasive actions of others. In life's journey, most people prefer ease to effort. We prefer being pampered rather than prodded. We prefer happiness to havoc. We desire comfort to challenge, repose to responsibility, security to sacrifice, and pleasure to pain. Most of all, we do not want problems or struggles. We prefer privileges. The teachings from Jesus in this passage often provoke difficulties, hardships, and misunderstandings. But they also build bridges to deeper relationships between people. These teachings are meant to bring healing, wholeness, and redemption when properly followed.

Hans Kung, a Catholic theologian, observed this about the passage:

> Jesus then did not demand and still less did he set in motion a politico-social revolution. What he did set going was a decidedly *non-violent revolution*: a revolution emerging from man's innermost and secret nature, from the personal center, from the heart of man, into society. There was to be no continuing in the old ways, but a radical change in man's thinking and a conversion (Greek, *metanoia*) away from all forms of selfishness, toward God and his fellow men. The real alien powers, from which man had to be liberated, were not the hostile world powers

but the forces of evil: hatred, injustice, dissension, violence, all human selfishness, and also suffering, sickness and death. There had to be therefore a changed awareness, a new way of thinking, a new scale of values. The evil that had to be overcome lay not only in the system, in the structures, but in man. Inner freedom had to be established and this would lead to freedom from external powers. Society had to be transformed through the transformation of the individual.[2]

The key fact here is that Jesus' teachings are not for the world at large. These are not teachings that any person can apply. Jesus is directing these teachings to people who are converted to him and his way. These are the radical demands for one who is Jesus' disciple. It is foolish for us to expect the world to be able to put these teachings into practice. But they are the teachings Jesus requires of his disciples. As another writer, Harry Emerson Fosdick, once wrote, Jesus "was deliberately presenting a way of life so demanding that no legalism could define it, no unredeemed heart practice it, no saint perfectly fulfill it."[3] Begin then with the awareness that Jesus Christ directs this teaching to his disciples. Only those who are his followers can truly live by this standard. Even for Christians, it will not be easy.

Going the First Mile

Let's see if we can understand what Jesus is trying to tell us here. First, I think we need to back up a step. Before we can go the second mile, give somebody our second tunic, or turn the other cheek, we first have to take the blow on one side of our face, go the first mile, and give away our first tunic. Most of us are unwilling to go even that far. Many of us have never taken that first step. We can't leap to the second mile before we go the first mile. What is the first mile? The first mile is the mile of obligation, responsibility, and duty. Each of us needs to learn that our cheeks may be hit occasionally, or we may have to give away one piece of clothing or go the first mile before we can take the next step. Many of us are unwilling to go that initial mile of duty, responsibility, and obligation. The first mile is to do the things that are your clear responsibility and your duty to perform. If you neglect these, you cannot truly go the second mile, turn the other cheek, or give away your topcoat.

Several years ago, Bill Jones, a dynamic preacher from New York, came to Southern Seminary and told about an experience he had when he was a small boy and went to visit his grandfather's farm. Being a city boy, this was the first time he had ever been to a farm. He and his grandfather got up bright and early the first day he was there and fed the chickens, milked the cows, slopped the hogs, chopped some wood, and then, after two hours, came back to the house and sat down for breakfast. The little boy looked over at his grandfather and said, "Granddaddy, we have really put in a hard day's work, haven't we?" "Son," his grandfather said, "we haven't done the real work yet. We have only done the chores. The real work lies before us out in the fields."

There are chores all around us that wait to be done. There are a lot of obligations lying at our doorsteps that we need to do first before we move to other responsibilities. We know that we should not commit adultery. But the first mile is found in Jesus' advice that we must overcome the lust in our hearts. Before we worry about killing somebody, Jesus says, we need to focus on the first mile of overcoming the hate and anger that we hold toward others. We must go the first step before we can be concerned about the next. The first mile, the first cheek, and the undergarment symbolize the way of working on the interior spirit.

How Do We Respond?

Suppose that you are pushed to the point of deciding whether you will go the second mile, turn the other cheek, or give your other coat. How do you respond? This demand is answered by returning more than is expected, more than is necessary, more than self-love, more than what is required by duty or obligation. It is not simply saying, "I will do harder work" or "I will be nice to Mrs. Smith." Jesus' way is much more demanding. We go the extra mile or turn the other cheek or give the outer coat out of love and a desire to be more like Christ.

The way of "turning the other cheek" and "the second mile" and "the outer coat" is undertaken voluntarily. Nobody can force us to take that step. We do it out of our sense of commitment to Christ and the Christ-like way. We can't be compelled to do it. We turn the other cheek because we feel that in doing so we can overcome evil with good. It is a voluntary act that we undertake to follow in the footsteps of our Lord. This doesn't mean it is easy. It can be difficult. But we have chosen a higher way than responding to evil with more evil.

When I was a summer student missionary in the Hawaiian Islands many years ago, I had the opportunity to go to the island of Molokai. For many years a leper colony has been located there, and one day I stood a hill that overlooked the leper colony. I remembered a story I had read about a young priest who visited there. The first day he was there he stood up and greeted the people by saying, "Friends, I come today to greet you in the name of Jesus Christ." Several years later, after he had contracted leprosy himself, he stood up to preach at the colony and said, "Fellow lepers, I greet you in the name of Jesus Christ." No one could have made him go there. Nobody could force him to work there, but, out of a sense of grace and love, he voluntarily went there to minister to those people in the name of Christ.

I have seen many other Christians do similar things on a different level of service. I remember a retired school principal named Hazel Bramm. I can still see Hazel, at eighty years old, trudging alone through the snow with her high boots as she came to church to tutor men who had never learned to read. She saw that as a challenge and her way of serving God. No one made her do it. We had people in one of my congregations who served God through our nursing home ministry, our HUGG Program, our Stephen Ministry, our Deacon Family Ministry, and in many other ways. These people voluntarily took the responsibility of caring for others and ministering to them. Nobody forced them to do this. They did it voluntarily because it was a way they showed the love of God.

More than Anyone Will Expect

As Christ followers, we also attempt to go the second mile, to turn the other cheek, or to give the other coat because it is more than anybody will ever expect. We expect often to give back in kind what we have received. That seems to be the natural way. A man stood still one day and was hit on one cheek and then he turned his head. His opponent quickly hit him on the other cheek. The man got up and brushed himself off. He then hit the other guy as hard as he could and said, "My Lord only said to turn the other cheek. He didn't tell me what to do after that." But that man misunderstood Jesus' teaching. Unfortunately, many of us have that attitude. "I'll turn the other cheek, but then I'll hit the other person as soon as I can and as hard as I can after that."

Learning about the Unexpected Way

Jesus is calling his disciples to a way that is so unexpected that it will catch others off guard. It will be so radical and startling that they won't understand it. Many expect us to retaliate in the same way they act toward us. Jesus has called us to a higher way.

We learn this approach from Jesus Christ, the master of the unexpected way. He was constantly interrupted by people, and he responded by doing unexpected things. When the man was lowered through the roof, Jesus was preaching to a crowd. The man disturbed Jesus' teaching, but Jesus met the man's need and taught an even greater lesson than with words alone. When the woman who was taken in adultery was cast at his feet, Jesus was asked whether or not she should be stoned. He did the unexpected thing. "He that is without sin," he said, "let him cast the first stone." When Jesus encountered the demoniac, he brought to that man unexpected healing and love. When he met Zacchaeus, who was up in a tree, rather than rejecting him Jesus went to the man's home for lunch and changed his life for good. When he met a woman at the well in Samaria, rather than saying, "I don't have anything to do with Samaritan women," he talked to her about her life and God.

We learn from Jesus Christ that our lives will constantly be interrupted. People will cross our paths, needs will confront us, individuals will ask for help. As Christians, we seek to meet those needs, and we may respond in unexpected ways. You and I probably will never have someone stone us, force us to go another mile, hit us on the cheek, or demand our coat—but we will be insulted, we will be misunderstood, and we will be resented. The way of a Christian is to respond in grace and love. Where there is insult, one returns kindness. Where there is rejection, one seeks to return graciousness. Where there is hostility, one seeks to return calmness and joy. Where there is unlovable behavior, a Christian seeks to reach out and show love. We seek to do the unexpected. It is the higher way of Christ.

The Way of Reconciliation

Why should Christians respond in this way? These words were not meant to be impractical or idealistic teachings. They were meant to be applied to life. Jesus wants us to follow a way that will bring reconciliation in the lives of people. Our desire should not be to destroy other people. We don't want to hurt them. We want to redeem them through the love of Christ. We are ambassadors of reconciliation. If Jesus Christ our Lord died for others, how can any Christian call a person for whom Christ died an enemy? Will Christ's death be in vain? The way you and I respond to other people with love can help them experience the love of Christ.

Unfortunately, even in our own lives as Christians, hatred is often present. When hatred is present in our attitude, we must ask if we are really trying to be like the Christ we follow. Hate cannot destroy hate. Only love can destroy hate. If you and I return hate to those who hate us, then we are only reflecting their image. We are then pulled into their way. We echo their tone. We mirror their approach. We give back only what we have received. But when you and I learn to love, we destroy the fire of their hatred. We give them no fuel to burn. Hatred cannot live when confronted by love. Love is the way of Christ, and love destroys hate because it transforms it with a higher way. Our behavior should not be determined by others. Let Christ set the direction.

Clarence Jordan, the founder of Koinonia Farm in Americus, Georgia, was a PhD graduate in Greek from Southern Seminary. When he founded Koinonia, he soon received a great deal of ridicule and hostility because his farm was completely integrated. While rigid segregation existed elsewhere, people of all races worked together on the farm.

One day Jordan went to the Sumter County livestock sale to buy some calves. He looked up and saw a man coming in the door who was the community's arch segregationist. Jordon knew what would happen next. Being a large man, he tried to bend down to see if he could avoid this man. But the man saw him and came straight over to him. "Here's that old Jordan fellow, folks! We ain't killed him yet, but we can kill him now. We got him here by hisself." Then, according to Jordan, the man began to pour forth some of the worst profanity he had ever heard. The man spoke about Jordan's canine ancestry and pedigree and used other negative images to describe what he thought of him.

Jordan simply stood there and listened as the man talked. He noticed that the man had no teeth he could knock out. But he could see his tonsils moving, and he said that he really wanted to do a public tonsillectomy on that man. Even so, he stood there and listened and did nothing. After the farmer had finished and walked away, another old farmer, who was sitting near him and seemed to wince every time the other farmer cursed Jordan, came over and asked, "You know what?" Jordan thought another attack was about to begin. But the man said, "I want to know how come you didn't hit that little fellow. You could have whooped him with one arm tied behind your back." "I think that is a correct appraisal of the situation," Jordan said. "Yes, I could have." "Well, how come you didn't hit him?" the farmer asked. "For two reasons," Jordan said. "If I'd hit that little segregationist, everyone in this sale barn would have jumped me and mopped the floor up with me. And I just didn't want my wife to be married to a mop. But the real reason," he continued, "was that I'm trying to be a follower of Jesus Christ and he taught me to love my enemies." "Is that what it means to be a Christian?"

the old farmer asked. Jordan said that the two of them sat down and then talked about what it means to be a Christian.[4]

It is easy sometimes to flex our muscles. We can be bigger and stronger and maybe even smarter than someone else. But is it Christian to use our strength and wisdom to destroy another person? Jesus Christ has called us not to the way of hatred but to the way of love and grace. This way often gets difficult.

Booker T. Washington once said, "I will never let any man reduce my soul to the level of hatred." We reach for a higher way. We seek to overcome evil with good. We reach out with the love of Christ in our lives and touch evil and hatred with love. "Love suffers long; love bears all things; love endures all things," Paul writes (1 Cor 13). When the higher way is part of one's life, then this kind of love literally does overcome evil. It may suffer when it challenges evil. It may be distorted, misunderstood, and abused, but ultimately love will be triumphant in the world because hate only begets hatred. Love will win because it is the higher, better way. As the Apostle Paul has reminded us, "Do not be overcome by evil but overcome evil with good" (Rom 12:21). Those of us who are genuinely Christian will attempt to live the Christ-like way and follow Jesus. It won't be easy, but Jesus never said taking up one's cross and following him was easy.

O God, we confess that often we want the easy way and the way of no effort. But help us to follow our Lord who calls us to a higher way, a way of love and the way of reconciliation. Teach us how to wage peace and to love our enemies, how to turn the other cheek, how to give others their rights and be less concerned about our own rights, and how to go the second mile as we follow our Lord, who gave this message not only in words but in his living and in his dying. Amen.

Notes

1. Anton S. LaVey, *The Satanic Bible* (Secaucus: University Press, 1969) 33.

2. Hans Kung, *On Being Christian* (Garden City NY: Doubleday & Co., 1976) 191.

3. Harry Emerson Fosdick, *The Man from Nazareth* (New York: Harper & Row, 1949) 106.

4. Dallas Lee, ed., *The Substance of Faith and Other Cotton Patch Sermons of Clarence Jordan* (New York: Association Press, 1972) 72–73.

4

How Can I Keep from Judging Others?

Matthew 7:1-5

Sally was a beautiful, bright, vivacious young woman who was a sophomore in high school. She was popular with boys and girls alike. One day some friends at school became jealous of her popularity and began to spread rumors about her. They said that she took drugs and gave sexual favors to any boy who came along. Soon Sally noticed that the friends with whom she spent time began to shun and ignore her. Her parents observed that she seemed to be depressed, but they did not know why. One morning Sally's parents called her to breakfast, but she did not respond. They went to her room and found her dead with a note and an empty bottle of pills beside her body. She killed herself because of gossip and untruths that were spread by supposed friends.

On the brighter side, there was a young teenage lad who had not done well in high school. He was admitted into a small junior college on probation. There was one professor at that school who did not like this young man and did everything he could to try to see that he flunked out of college. This professor could not see any hope or potential in the young man. But another professor could see his potential. This professor worked with the young man, helped him overcome some of his deficiencies from high school, and did some remedial education with him. The remarkable fact was that this young man did well in junior college, went on to senior college, graduated with honors, and later got a doctor's degree. He did well because there was somebody whose judgment encouraged and supported him.

Judgments of All Kinds

If we are honest, we must admit that Jesus' statement in Matthew 7:1-5 is troublesome. Jesus said, "Judge not lest you be judged." But we judge all the time, don't we? We make judgments by the kinds of clothes we buy, the food we eat, the cars we drive, the houses we live in, the television shows we watch or don't watch, the books we read or don't read, the places we go for vacations, the friends we make, the person we choose for our spouse. We make judgments all the time. We can't avoid them completely. But some of our judgments are based on the color of a person's skin, their educational level, where they're from, what part of town they live in, the size of their bank account, what college they attended, or the kind of house they have. We judge people by their Southern or Yankee accents or their Virginia brogue. We make judgments on people harshly and quickly.

Few of us are guilty of the big sins like murder, stealing, or adultery, but every one of us is guilty of the sin of judging others unjustly. We have committed this sin across the dinner table, over the backyard fence, on the golf course, over the bridge club table, while walking the halls at school or church, or even over the telephone. Our tongues have wagged. Our eyes have flashed. We have assassinated someone's character, pointed fingers, and hurled spears of prejudgment. We have talked about other people and made hasty, uninformed judgments.

Jesus commanded us, "Judge not." But we want to exclaim, "Wait a minute, Jesus. You said that Herod was an 'old fox.' You warned us to beware of the 'leaven of the scribes and Pharisees.' You called them 'whitewashed tombs.' You told us to be careful about people who dressed in sheep's clothing but were wolves in a sheep's skin. You told us not to be like people who seek the first seats at a banquet. You instructed us that we would know your disciples 'by their fruits.'"

In his commandment against judgment, did Jesus mean we are not to have any discrimination at all? Of course not! The Greek word for "judge" is the root for our word "critic." The word "judge" here means "censor another with unjust criticism." Do not judge someone else quickly, harshly, and without thorough knowledge. Do not make hypocritical judgments.

Improper Judgments

Why are our judgments often so wrong? It is important to remember that we are all fallible. None of us are inerrant in our judgments of others. Why? For one thing, we simply never have all the facts. No one can possibly know everything about every situation. Look at some of the wrong judgments that have been made in history.

One man wrote the following words about George Washington: "The present occupant of the White House is little better than a murderer. He is treacherous in private friendships, a hypocrite in public life, an imposter who has either abandoned all good principles or else never had any." Lincoln's "Gettysburg Address" was described by one newspaper editor as "a silly little speech that will soon be forgotten." When William Wordsworth published one of his first poems, a critic wrote, "This will never do." The Wright brothers' first flight never even made the newspapers. Many thought they were a couple of "boys" playing. When the Beatles began to sing in Liverpool, many did not think their music would be taken seriously. They thought the band members were a bunch of funny-looking guys. How many times have people made quick and wrong judgments about scientific discoveries, music, art, plays, novels, movies, actors, writers, or something else? We see only partially.

Unaware of All the Facts

No one ever has all the facts. Too often we listen to rumor, innuendo, and half-truth, and we jump to conclusions. We make decisions on inadequate or false information. During the McCarthy era, a person's career or reputation could be destroyed simply by raising the question, "Isn't Joe Smith a person who is associated with communists?" They didn't have to say that Joe Smith *was* a communist. By mere association, he was slandered, judged guilty, and often lost his job. Someone might ask a question in the office: "Is it true that Mary and Tom are having an affair?" Later, when this person is confronted with the accusation, she may reply, "I didn't really say they were having an affair. I was just asking a question." But the way she asked her question destroyed the character of two people. "Why does our teacher seem so dull and grim today?" the students asked. They did not know that he had just buried his father, and it was his first time to be back in class. We make hasty judgments without all the facts.

Samuel Crockett wrote a book titled *The Stickit Minister*.[1] The people who live in the community where the story is set call the older brother a blockhead because he has left the university and come home to work in the fields. They label him the "Stickit Minister." But they are uninformed. His father is in poor health and can no longer run the farm. The older brother left the university and came back to run the farm so his younger brother could go to school. There are not enough funds for both of them to go to college, so the older brother stays at home and works in the fields and gives up his dreams of being a scholar. He renounces his calling to the ministry because of his father's poor health and to make way for his brother to go to school instead. His hard labor in the fields is not the work of a person who is a failure; it's the sign of a magnanimous spirit.

Judgments are often rendered without people knowing all the facts. How can we ever really understand another person's motives? We don't know what is going on in that person's heart. How could we possibly know? People might look at a shabbily dressed woman and ask, "Why does she dress like that? Why doesn't she buy some decent-looking clothes?" But they don't know that she cannot afford any more clothes. All her money goes to take care of her sick mother and her small children. "Why doesn't he give more to the church?" a person asks. "Look at the job he has. Why doesn't he do more?" People who ask such things don't realize that the man is not only taking care of his own family but also of his mother and father, his widowed sister, and his brother who has lost his job.

I had a friend in college who often seemed to be melancholy. Many people made harsh judgments about him. I didn't know why he always seemed sad until one day we talked privately and he told me that his father was an alcoholic who had abused him, his mother, and his brother and sister. All his life he struggled with the darkness hidden in his own closet. How quickly and carelessly we judge another person without knowing the hurts, problems, and difficulties they have to bear. Some old lines express this truth well: "There's so much good in the worst of us, / And so much bad in the best of us, / That it hardly becomes any of us, / To talk about the rest of us."

How true these lines are. The old saying is correct as well: "You should never judge another person until you have walked in his shoes for two months." If we only knew what was going on in the life of somebody else—what burdens, perplexities, pains, or sorrows—maybe our judgments of them would be entirely different.

In the novel *Not as a Stranger* by Morton Thompson, a young physician, Dr. Marsh, goes to the president of the local medical association and accuses an older doctor of malpractice.[2] The president listens to him and then discourages him from continuing with his charges. But Dr. Marsh insists that he is going to press ahead. The president then leans across his desk and observes, "I am going to suggest this to you—that if you persist in bringing formal charges, then be sure of one thing. Don't ever, as long as you live, make a single mistake." It is easy to jump to conclusions about someone without knowing what may be happening in that person's life.

Not Impartial in Judgment

We are also not impartial in our judgments. Let's be honest: every person has some prejudice. We pre-judge another person and do not try to determine whether what we have heard is true. Prejudice may blind us from seeing the gifts another person has. I heard about a man who moved from a deep southern state into a northern section of the country to take over a supervisory position in a large firm. He was a very gifted, talented, and well-educated man. When he assumed his new position, he began to make some changes. The Northerners in the office did not like his Southern accent. They were opposed to the changes their boss was making, and several employees in the office started rumors. Innuendos began to float around. Soon everything the boss tried to do was blocked. All of his efforts were squelched. He became a nervous wreck. Business fell off. Finally, he had to resign his position, and the firm filed for bankruptcy. This all came about because of rumors that were started by a few people in the firm who simply didn't like the man's accent or the changes he had made. They were unwilling to give him a chance.

In Charles Schultz's *Peanuts* comic strip, Lucy is depicted giving Charlie Brown a tongue-lashing. "You are the sorriest, no-good, good-for-nothing person I know," she says. "You never do anything right. You always mess up." Next is a blank frame. Then she turns to him and asks, "Incidentally, Charlie Brown, how come I never hear you singing anymore?" Sometimes we level our criticism and improper judgments on others, and then we wonder why they behave as they do. Our self-interest and expectation that everyone else should see things from our perspective keep us from making sound judgments. Remember: our judgments are never infallible.

Judging May Boomerang

We must also be aware that our judging may have a way of returning to judge us. A lot of the criticism of others is really self-judgment. Psychologists say that often the things we detest most in other people may actually be our response to the weaknesses we see in ourselves. As the old saying goes, "It takes one to know one." "He's lazy," we say. "She's good-for-nothing." "He's immature." We can only say we know about these factors by revealing our own acquaintance with them. "The truth," Theodore H. Robinson notes, "is that no man can pass an opinion on any other person or thing without at the same time recording a judgment on himself. He 'gives himself away' more by his criticism than by any other act or word."[3]

Sometimes what we despise in others is a reflection on what we see buried deep within us. Ralph Waldo Emerson expressed it this way:

> A man cannot speak but he judges himself. With his will, or against his will, he draws his portrait to the eye of his companions by every word. Every opinion reacts on him who utters it. It is a thread-ball thrown at a mark, but the other end remains in the thrower's bag. Or, rather, it is a harpoon thrown at the whale, unwinding, as it flies, a coil of cord in the boat, and if the harpoon is not good, or not well thrown, it will go high to cut the steersman in twain or to sink the boat.[4]

Often the words of judgment with which we lash out at someone else come back on us and show other people a weakness that is within ourselves.

Jesus said, "You be careful how you judge others, because the standard of judgment that you use to measure other people will be the one by which your own life is measured" (Matt 7:1-2). It is simply one of the facts of life. Sometimes the people who are always complaining about someone else gossiping or about another person cheating or voicing some other matter become suspect themselves. People begin to watch these individuals to see if they are guilty of the things they accuse other people of doing. If a person always expresses concern about somebody else's honesty, soon others begin to wonder about that person's honesty. If Mr. Smith is always talking about somebody else gossiping, some may begin to listen to what *he* is saying about other people.

Hypocritical Judgments

Jesus expressed concern about hypocritical judging. Here is old "log-eye" who has a huge log sticking out his eye. While this log is protruding out of his eye, he approaches another and complains about the tiny sawdust speck he sees in their eye. Jesus says, "Old log-eye, you quit worrying about somebody else's eye. You get busy taking out the log that is in your own eye." Our primary effort in life is not to be concerned about the faults of others but to look at the faults within ourselves.

A man drove into a new community and stopped a farmer who was working in a field and commented, "We are thinking of moving to this town. What kinds of folks are here?" "What kinds of folks are in the community where you came from?" the farmer asked. "They were the sorriest people

I have ever lived with in my life. They were wishy-washy, lazy, and good-for-nothing," the stranger replied. "Oh, you will find the same kinds of folks here," the farmer observed. A few moments later another man stopped his car and said, "We are thinking of moving to this community. What kinds of people live here?" "What kinds of folks were in the community where you came from?" the farmer asked. "They were wonderful people," the man said. "They were good neighbors and we loved it." "Come on to our community," the farmer replied. "You will find the same kinds of people here." We often find what we look for. Life gives back what we put into it. The way we judge others is our own measure for judgment. Our judgments reflect us. We are judged by our own judgments. Dietrich Bonhoeffer expressed it this way:

> Every idle word which we think so little of betrays our lack of respect for our neighbor, and shows that we place ourselves on a pinnacle above him and value our own lives higher than his. The angry word is a blow struck at our brother, a stab at his heart: It seeks to hit, to hurt and to destroy. A deliberate insult is even worse, for we are then openly disgracing our brother in the eyes of the world, and causing others to despise him. With our hearts burning with hatred, we seek to annihilate his moral and material existence. We are passing judgment on him, and that is murder. And the murderer will himself be judged.[5]

The way you judge others determines how you will be judged.

Our religion is ultimately one of grace. Judgment belongs to God alone. Aren't you thankful that God has not passed judgment on you based entirely on the way you live and act? Salvation is by grace, not by works. We would all be in real trouble if our salvation was based on our actions. God alone can ultimately judge someone rightly.

Look for Potential in Others

Try to see with clear eyes. This is one of the significant points in our text. The "log" or "speck" is a foreign object in the eye and needs to be removed so a person can see clearly. When some people look at others, especially people like "log-eye," all they see is the "speck" or splinter" in everyone else's eyes. They can't see the real person for the "speck." However, when Jesus looked at people, he saw not the "speck" but the potential within them. He looked at Matthew and saw not a tax collector but a faithful disciple. He looked at Thomas and saw not only his doubts but also his faithfulness. He looked at Peter and saw not merely his quick temper and anger but also his courage and faith. He looked at the woman accused of adultery and saw not a harlot but a committed disciple. He looked at Saul and saw not a narrow Pharisee but a missionary to the Gentiles.

Jesus looked at a person and saw the real individual when the evil was exorcised from them. He was constantly seeking to make people whole. He cast out evil spirits and demons to bring healing and wholeness to those in need. He saw what they could be. He did not see the "speck" but what people could be when made whole.

See Others as Real People

Remember that we all are sisters and brothers in Christ. Learn to look upon others as real people. Too often we see other people primarily in terms of their function. This perspective views others as "things" or "its." We see people only as a waiter, a policeman, a doctor, an attorney, an accountant, a preacher, a janitor, or whatever. But worse, we see some people only as a harlot, a cheat, a thief, a liar, lazy, no good, weak, or a bum. We don't see these people as real human beings. We must remember that they are people whom God loves and has come to redeem. We need to see as our Lord sees. "Jesus' teaching is not a strategy for success in this-worldly relationships," Eugene Boring reminds us, "but a call to live in the light of the dawning kingdom of God."[6]

When we see other people as our brothers and sisters, then we strive not to hurt or insult them but instead to love and help them. Let us practice love and praise. Jesus has called us to reach out and help others who are in need and guide them into a deeper, more mature faith.

One day a young daughter wrapped her arms around her father's neck. She was hugging him tightly and the father was hugging her back. But the mother, who was standing nearby, noticed that as Mary hugged her father, she stuck out her tongue at her brother, who was standing behind her. "Mary," her mother said, "you can't hug your father and stick your tongue out at your brother at the same time. Remember your father loves both of you." That is almost a biblical paraphrase, isn't it? If you and I claim we love God, then we will also love our brothers and sisters. We will reach out to embrace all people.

Ask Three Questions

Ask yourself three simple questions before you attempt to reach conclusions about the actions of another person. (1) Is it true? Is it really true or is it just a rumor? Is it fact? (2) Is it necessary? Is it really necessary to tell somebody else what you have heard? (3) Is it kind? If you report what you have heard or seen, will your words help this person or hurt him?

Jesus said that the judgment we use to judge other people is how we will be judged. Don't be concerned about the tiny speck or fault or weakness that you see in somebody else, but look at the big log—the huge weakness—in your own life. Then get busy trying to change your own faults. Paul, writing to the Philippians' church, concluded his epistle this way:

> And now, my friends, all that is true, all that is noble, all that is just and pure, all that is lovable and gracious, whatever is excellent and admirable, fill all your thoughts with these things. The lessons I taught you, the traditions I have passed on, all that you heard me say or saw me do, put into practice; and the God of peace will be with you. (Phil 4:8-9)

And the God of peace will be with you and me too.

Notes

1. S. R. Crockett, *The Stickit Minister* (London: T. Fisher Unwin, 1894).

2. Morton Thompson, *Not as a Stranger* (New York: Scribner, 1954).

3. Theodore H. Robinson, *The Gospel of Matthew* (New York: Doubleday, Duran & Co, 1928) 60.

4. Ralph W. Emerson, *Essays: First Series* (Boston: Houghton, Mifflin, and Company, 1883).

5. Dietrich Bonhoeffer, *The Cost of Discipleship* (London: SCM Press, 1959) 116.

6. M. Eugene Boring, "The Gospel of Matthew," *The New Interpreter's Bible* (Nashville: Abingdon Press, 1995) 211.

5

The Danger of Anger

Matthew 5:21-24

Suddenly, over the buzz of grocery store noise, the other customers heard a woman say angrily to her child, "I've told you a dozen times to stop doing that!" A loud smack was heard, and a child began to cry boisterously.

A conference was being held in an office downtown. First the neck and then the face of the boss got redder and redder. Those present could see a vein in his neck as it began to pulsate rapidly. The boss, blowing his stack, stated his point with great fury and underscored it with all kinds of obscenities.

We see or read about uncontrolled anger all the time.

We witness the fury of anger when we read in the paper that a husband has abused his wife or a child has to go to the hospital because a mother or father lost control of their temper and beat the child. We see uncontrolled anger at a ballgame when a player is shown standing face to face with a referee furiously arguing his point. Unfortunately, we see anger all around us. And we have to confess that we also know about it firsthand.

There are times when you, like me, fly off the handle, blow your stack, hit the ceiling, lose your cool, go into a rage, or become mad as a hornet. Anger seems to be too much a part of our lives. In the Old Testament, the word for anger depicts a person whose "nose burns." We have all seen times when more than the nose was burning on an angry person. Sometimes the word in Hebrew is "a pregnant nose," which indicates the swollen nature of anger. In an ancient painting, anger was depicted as a man with a knife in his mouth, a vial of poison in one hand, and his other arm in a sling from some previous confrontation. Anger is too familiar to us all.

Hear again the words from our text as recorded in Phillips' translation:

"You have heard that it was said to people in the old days, 'Thou shalt not murder,' and anyone who does so must stand his trial. But I say to you that anyone who is angry with his brother must stand his trial; anyone who contemptuously calls his brother a fool must face the Supreme Court; and anyone who looks down on his brother as a lost soul is himself heading straight for the fires of destruction. So that if, while you are offering your gift at the altar, you should remember that your brother has something against you, you must leave your gift there before the altar and go away. Make your peace with your brother first, then come offer your gift." (Matt 5:21-24)

This passage is included among the difficult sayings of Jesus because he seems to say that if we get angry enough, our anger can cause us to go to hell. This ought to trouble us, because who among us doesn't get angry? We also need to know that most scholars believe the phrase "without cause" was not part of the original text and that a scribe added it later. Jesus doesn't put any qualifying restriction on justifying one's anger. If we are capable of feeling anger that leads to our destruction, maybe we need to reflect on it a few moments.

Anger as a Normal Part of Human Nature

Let's begin with the acknowledgment that anger is a normal part of our nature. We get angry just like we get tired or sad. It is a normal part of being human. But there are also destructive forms of anger. This kind of anger is not healthy. We have all seen how devastating this anger can be. We have witnessed the damage anger does to relationships, individuals, marriages, churches, businesses, and even countries. There is normal anger and there is abnormal anger. Winston Churchill once heard one of his opponents in the Parliament direct a hot-tempered tirade against him. After the man finished, Churchill stood up and said, "Our honorable colleague should by now have trained himself not to generate more indignation than he has the capacity to hold." Too many of us get far angrier than a situation warrants.

I like the expression Wayne Oates often used: "A person should never throw his weight around until he has first weighed in." The same is true with anger. We need to think about our anger. Before you unleash it with such fury, ask yourself: Is it really worth it? Is it necessary? What will be its effect? What will it do for me or to other people? Is it worthwhile?

The Anger of Jesus

Charles Jefferson wrote these interesting lines years ago:

> So prone is anger to mix itself with base and unlovely elements, and so frequently does it stir up the mud at the bottom of the soul, that it has been often classed among the vices as a passion which is always ignoble and therefore to be condemned, resisted, strangled. . . . It is not easy to free one's self from the feeling that anger has something sinful in it, or that if anger is not actually sinful, it is at any rate unlovely, a defect or flaw in conduct, a deformity in character from which the lovers of the beautiful and good may wisely pray to be delivered. It is because of this assumption that anger is in its essence sinful that many persons find it impossible to think of Jesus in an angry mood.[1]

If we read the New Testament, however, we will discover that there is not only a meek and mild Jesus but also an angry Jesus. Jesus was the Lamb of God, but there were other times when Jesus was the Lion of Judah. Sometimes Jesus was tender and compassionate. But at other times Jesus was terrible in his scorn, and his wrath was almost unbelievable in its fury. Jesus chose words to describe some of the scribes and Pharisees that resounded with harshness: "you serpents," "you generation of vipers," "you white-washed tombs," and "you children of hell." Whether you like it or not, there were times when Jesus directed angry, harsh, fierce, condemning words at certain people. When we read the New Testament, though, we discover that the anger of Jesus was never about something personal that had been directed toward him. Selfish concern never prompted his anger. When he took a whip in his hand and walked into the temple and knocked over the money-changers' tables, his anger was directed toward those who were distorting what the temple of God was supposed to be. His anger was directed at those who exploited the poor, the needy, the hungry, the outcasts, women, widows, and children.

A Proper Place for Anger

There is a proper place in our lives for anger. In fact, if Christians never get angry at anything, then something is wrong with us. Not being angry at certain things may even be sinful. If you and I are confronted by the exploitation of the poor and underprivileged, if we see that people are victims of racism, if we witness hunger, disease, poverty, child abuse, suffering, and crime and don't get angry enough to want to change these conditions, then something is wrong with us. "Righteous anger is usually not about oneself," Archbishop Desmond Tutu notes. "It is about those whom one sees being harmed and whom one wants to help."[2]

As Christians, we need to direct our anger toward the causes of these conditions and seek to correct them or change them for the better. E. Stanley Jones has voiced a prayer that all Christians need to pray: "O Christ of the whip and the flashing eye, give us an inward hurt at the wrong done to others, but save us from personal resentments, for they destroy us. Amen."[3] Yes, there is a proper time for anger. Anger needs to be directed against people who hurt and harm others needlessly. This kind of anger can help the church reclaim its birthright as it responds to T. S. Eliot's lines, "In the juvescence of the year / Came Christ the tiger."[4] This kind of explosive power can enable Christians to stand up for justice against tyranny, oppression, hatred, and bigotry. The church needs to be angry at injustice and oppression and not be afraid to speak out against it.

Called to a Higher Way

In our text Jesus is focused not on righteous anger that brings needed change but on soul-crushing anger that ruins individuals. He is calling us to a higher way in his kingdom. This teaching is directed to Christians, those who have committed their lives to be a part of the kingdom of God. It is obvious that not every Christian can always live by Jesus' high standard. Even so, Christians are summoned to seek the higher way. Jesus begins by challenging the teachings of the scribes and Pharisees. "You have heard that it has been said to you, but now I say to you . . . ," he says. In Jesus' day, many people could not read. They received instructions about the Scriptures from the oral teachings of scribes and Pharisees. Those authorities said, "This is what the Scriptures mean." And then Jesus said, "You may have been told a particular meaning for the commandment, 'you shall not kill,' but I am telling you that the scribes and Pharisees have not correctly interpreted the law." He noted that the Pharisees had weakened the law's demands. The law is not limited by our actions. The truth is that the law reaches beyond the apparent deeds of human beings. Jesus pushes our understanding of the law to the motive behind each action.

Examining Our Intention

Jesus underscored the point that will and action are interrelated. He stressed that a person's intention, desire, or thought can be sinful because they may lead to action. A few verses later Jesus will speak about adultery, observing that it is not limited to the physical act but can also be committed within one's heart. Behind the action is the impure or hostile thought. Jesus is not saying that murder and thinking about murder are the same thing. I don't know anybody who would rather be killed than hated. Obviously the two are not equal. But Jesus is telling us that hatred leads to murder. The thought, idea, desire, or intention leads to the action. We must examine both the root and the fruit of any action. Courts of law are concerned with acts of crime. God's judgment is not limited to the acts.

Jesus states further that the intention leads to verbal contempt. My negative or cruel words toward another person arise from within my heart and mind. Jesus draws on some strange words here. He refers to the word "raca," an Aramaic word that scholars have had difficulty translating. It has been translated variously as "imbecile," "you worthless person," "blockhead," "brainless idiot," or "dumb ox." Think of the worst insult you could say to somebody, and that is what this word implies.

An Ascending Scale in Attitude

Jesus presents an ascending scale of attitudes towards others. A person begins with long-lasting anger. This anger might lead him before the local judgment bar of the circuit court. Next comes a worse kind of anger that motivates contemptuous action toward another person. The sin of contempt is under the judgment of the Jewish Supreme Court, the Sanhedrin. Then the person moves to the worst stage of all, seeking to ruin somebody's name and reputation. This sin of the worst insult receives the harshest judgment, the fire of Gehenna. To call someone a fool implies that the person is ungodly. The Old Testament has stated that "the fool has said in his heart that there is no God." To call another a fool is to destroy that person's reputation.

We often say, "Sticks and stones may break my bones, but words will never hurt me." But that is not true! We can recover from cuts and bruises caused by sticks and stones, but cruel words can destroy reputations and lives. The point is that all our thoughts and actions are under the judgment of God, even if they are not subject to human courts.

Degrading a Person's Character

Jesus reminds us here that when we insult people, we degrade their character. What we are doing is like murder because we destroy their reputation. Hurling such insults at others leads to their destruction, and no one will escape God's judgment for such action. Hell or Gehenna refers to the garbage dump outside of Jerusalem, the most vile, distasteful place the ancient Hebrew could imagine. It became a symbol for eternal torment. All of this affirms the destructive nature of the anger that lies behind an overt action.

The Boomerang Effect of Anger

Harboring anger not only harms others but can also destroy the self. Resentment can slowly but surely destroy a person who has anger and hatred buried deep within his or her heart. The anger that we bury deeply in our minds soon colors our attitude toward others. We find ourselves backed into a dead-end street of bitterness. Anger and hate are our daily companions. We notice that our anger has caused us to be bankrupt of joy. We no longer have a sense of the happiness of life; our minds are focused only on what we can do to hurt another person or get even or retaliate. Our desire for revenge is like a cancer in our souls. We cling to our resentments and anger until they destroy us.

I know a man whose wife tried to get him to go see a doctor because of an infection on his foot. But he said, "Ah, it will be okay. I don't think it's serious." He ignored it and put off going to the doctor until it was too late and his foot had to be amputated. While he ignored his problem, the infection continued to do its ghastly work. When we bury anger, resentment, and hostility deep down inside of us, it will steadily grow until its evil force colors our whole nature and personality.

Frederick Buechner has described the deadly efforts of anger this way:

> Of the Seven Deadly Sins, anger is probably the most fun. To lick your wounds, to smack your lips over grievances long passed, to roll over your tongue the prospect of bitter confrontations still to come, to savor to the last toothsome morsel both the pain you are given and the pain you are giving back—in many ways it is a feast fit for a king. The chief drawback is that what you are woofing down is yourself. The skeleton at the feast is you.[5]

Hostility toward others does not hurt them alone. This buried anger is a cancer that eats away at our very being. It likely harms us more than it does others.

Love as a Call to Reconciliation

Jesus issues a call to reconciliation. He says that you and I are supposed to be children of the kingdom of God. And if we are children in God's kingdom, we ought to learn to live together without engaging in anger, quarrels, and thoughts of retaliation. We ought to try to learn how to get along with one another. A sign of genuine Christianity is love for other people. It contradicts the definition of a Christian to spend time hating and fighting with others. If there is any evidence that we are not the authentic church as our Lord founded us to be, whether it is on the local or national level, it is when we are always fighting. What must God's judgment be upon a quarrelsome, angry church or religious institution? Our hostility reveals that we are far from what we are supposed to be as God's people. This is an absolute disgrace.

Anger Harms Our Worship

Hostility and hatred also interfere with our worship. When we come to our place of worship with our offerings for God, and, as we are sitting there we remember some fault, conflict, misunderstanding, or argument that we have with another, we are told to get up from our seats and go to make things right with that person. Whether it is something we remember doing to another or something he or she did to us, we must go set it right. We can't expect to worship God and hate other people. We can't really worship, Jesus says, because our hatred cuts us off from communing with God. In the Lord's Prayer, Jesus said to pray, "Father, forgive us our sins as we forgive those who have sinned against us."

Take Positive Action to Correct Anger

Jesus issues a strong word for positive action. If we come before God with our offering and remember a brother or sister whom we have harmed or who has harmed us, then we should do something about it. We should not keep harboring resentment, anger, and ill feelings. Instead, we should talk to that person and seek to make our relationship good again. Paul writes, "Be angry but sin not. Do not let the sun go down on your anger" (Eph 4:26). Have you ever thought what would happen in our churches, families, and other relationships if, every time we had a misunderstanding, quarrel, or some difference of opinion, we could immediately talk about it and settle it? I believe we would have fewer divorces, fewer splits in churches, fewer crimes, less business conflict, fewer fights at school, and less evidence of improper anger in general. Doesn't our uncontrolled anger reveal how far we are from being the church or part of the kingdom of God?

Listen to the words from 1 Corinthians that Paul writes in the thirteenth chapter:

> Love has good manners and does not pursue selfish advantage. It is not touchy. It does not keep an account of evil or gloat over the weakness of other people. On the contrary, it is happy with all good persons when truth prevails. Love knows no limits in its endurance, no end to its trust, no fading of its hope, it can outlast anything. It is, in fact, the one thing that will stand when all else has fallen. (1 Cor 13:4-8)

May God give us the grace to have such Christian love in our lives that we will indeed be able to love others even as God has loved us while we were still unlovely. May God give us the grace to be what he has called us to be.

Notes

1. Dalai Lama and Desmond Tutu (with Douglas Abrams) *The Book of Joy* (New York: Avery: An Imprint of Penguin Random House, 2016) 106.

2. Charles Jefferson, *The Character of Jesus* (New York: Thomas Y. Crowell & Co., 1908) 298–99.

3. E. Stanley Jones, *Victorious Living* (New York: Abingdon Press, 1936) 226.

4. T. S. Eliot, lines from "Gerontion."

5. Frederick Buechner, *Wishful Thinking* (New York: Harper & Row, 1976) 2.

6

How Can I Love My Enemies?

Matthew 5:43-44

Jesus' words that we are to love our enemies seem not only difficult but, if we are honest, impossible to put into practice. How, for example, do people who were freed from years of imprisonment by terrorists forgive their enemies? How do relatives who stand before the Vietnam Memorial in Washington, DC, love the enemies who killed their loved ones? How do the millions of Jews who saw their husbands, wives, children, and parents gassed, victimized, and tortured in Nazi concentration camps forgive those who did this? How do the Japanese who lived in Nagasaki and Hiroshima forgive the United States for dropping atomic bombs on them? How do the relatives of those who were killed in the terrorist attacks of 9/11 forgive those who were responsible for those acts?

Forgive Your Enemies

"Forgive your enemies" sounded difficult in the day when Jesus first uttered it. He was addressing a people who were at that moment enslaved by the Romans. Their fellow Jews were working with the Roman government to collect taxes from them. Jewish religious leaders often set up restrictions of the law so binding that no person who had any kind of ordinary job could possibly follow their rigid regulations.

Challenging Examples

In interpreting what he meant by loving one's enemies, Jesus gave several examples. If a person smacks you on the right cheek, which would have to be struck with the back of his hand, this would be a double insult. But Jesus said that they were to turn the other cheek as well. If a Roman soldier compelled you to carry his pack one mile, as you were walking down a road going about matters of your own, don't just go a mile but go two miles. If someone asks for your tunic, give him your cloak also. This would be like not giving him merely your shirt but your overcoat as well. Think how impossible these teachings must have sounded. (See chapter 3 above for more on this passage.)

Jesus' teachings seem to cut against common sense. "If there is anybody we ought to hate," his listeners must have thought, "it is certainly our enemies—especially the Romans." During war, and especially when a country is occupied by an enemy force, it is easy to arouse feelings of hatred. Hatred was easily stirred up in our country when we were at war with Germany and Japan. Think about your own feelings toward the people responsible for the 9/11 attacks when you read about their activities in the paper or hear about them on TV.

Who are Our Enemies?

Enemies are easy to define in wartime. Let's put wartime terrorists, murderers, and rapists aside for a moment and bring our enemies closer to home. Who is our enemy? Our enemy is anybody who hates us or who wishes us harm or injury through word or deed. An enemy comes closer and takes on a familiar face when we see an enemy as someone who may cause us difficulty and turmoil in our jobs or who makes our work miserable. Our enemy may be seen as someone who has caused us to go bankrupt; hurt our reputations through gossip or slander; told a half-truth about us; sought to cause us harm; or made fun of us, put us down, ridiculed us. An enemy may be someone who has closed the door of communication or who responds differently to us because she has misunderstood or misinterpreted something we said or did. All of us feel that we have encountered some kind of enemy in our lifetimes.

Why Should I Love My Enemy?

The more basic question seems to be, "*Why* should I love my enemy?" Why should we try to love somebody who hurts us, hates us, or causes us harm?

If you respond to a person who dislikes you or hates you with the same attitude he is directing toward you, you will soon find that your life is poisoned from within. Hatred is a self-destructive attitude. Jesus even said that the wells of anger and lust within us determine our outward behavior.

We need to make a distinction between hating things and hating people. We tend to identify a person with his or her vicious, destructive, or harmful behavior. It is easy to hate a murderer, rapist, or terrorist. Instead, let's direct our indignation to the root cause behind the evil rather than to the person who is committing the act of evil. We need to love the person and hate the evil. We need to overcome war, prostitution, prejudice, drugs, and other enemies, but not by hating the people involved in them.

Why should we love our enemy? We love our enemy because love is the only power that can change our enemy. Jesus was interested not in condemning a person but in saving him, making him whole. No prostitute was ever changed by someone treating her as a prostitute. No thief was ever changed by someone treating him as a thief. An enemy is not changed by our treating him as an enemy. Love is the power that can convert an enemy into a friend.

The Necessity of Forgiving

Why do we want to love? Because it is only in forgiving others that we are truly forgiven ourselves. This is what Jesus taught us in the Lord's Prayer: "Forgive us our trespasses as we forgive those who have trespassed against us." If you and I refuse to forgive others, we close the door to our own forgiveness by God.

Loving Does Not Equal Liking

We begin to love our enemy by realizing that we don't always have to like our enemy. There are things that our enemies do that we will never like. Who can like somebody who murders and rapes, robs and beats, hurts others with words, victimizes people, or is prejudiced against certain individuals? It is difficult to like these people. However, we are told not to like them but to love them.

The word *agape* is different from a sentimental concept of love. *Agape* means that we deliberately direct our will to accomplish what is best for our enemies. This kind of love is not based on emotion or sentiment. As I showed love to my children by directing my will to recognize and motivate the best within them, there were times when I had to deny them what they wanted. At times, I had to discipline them or put restraints on what they wanted to do. I had to correct or try to modify their behavior. I may not have liked what they did, but I continued to love my children. I also continue to love myself when I do some things that I don't like. Real love does not say it makes no difference what a person does. By an effort of my will—by loving other people—I try to bring about change in their lives.

Don't Identify a Person with His or Her Sins

Another way to love my enemy is by not identifying the person with his or her sins. I make a distinction between my *real* self and what I do. I need to do the same for others. I have to see the potential within others. If I refuse, I will never give someone a chance to change. Jesus looked at people and saw what they could be through grace and forgiveness. He saw Zacchaeus, a tax collector, who was one of the most despised people of his day. Yet he realized the difference it would make if he would follow Jesus and change his life. Jesus saw within the life of Mary Magdalene, an outcast of society, what she could become through transforming love. He saw within Saul, who was persecuting and executing Christians, a pioneering missionary.

What God Does for Us

We can learn to forgive our enemies when we begin to realize how often people do not understand their own actions. Jesus prayed on the cross, "Father, forgive them, for they know not what they do." The influence of friends, relatives, peer groups, community, social or national pressures, gangs, or other pressures cause us to act the way we do. Sometimes we do not really "know what we do." But thank God we can break free from this pressure and experience forgiveness. We can have the opportunity to start again.

Radical Forgiveness Identifies Us with God

Jesus told his disciples that if they learned to forgive their enemies, they would be children of the Most High (Luke 6:35). This kind of love reveals that we are like God the Father. Even if we are like the prodigal son and go into the farthest country of sin, God will forgive us when we say, "Father, I have sinned." Out of love, God extends grace that brings about forgiveness.

A Demanding Love

This kind of love is not easy. Its claim on our lives and attitude is demanding. The love that Jesus Christ models for us goes beyond anything we can imagine. This love demands the forgiveness of others, the unwillingness to cling to grudges or harbor hatred, and the goal of being "perfect" like God. Christ calls us to be unselfish, caring, patient, understanding, loving, and sacrificial. Jesus didn't say his way was easy. Loving our enemies is difficult and hard to accept. But it is at the heart of our faith. This teaching makes us realize how far we are from following our Lord's way.

7

When It's Hard to Forgive

Matthew 18:21-35

"It happened several years ago, three years ago to be precise," the white woman told me, "and our marriage has just never been the same since. He said he was sorry and would not do it again. But he broke our marriage vows. He committed adultery. I can't forget it! How can I ever forgive him?"

Time changes. A different time, a different face. "It happened so long ago," the black man said, "but it is as clear in my mind as though it were yesterday. That teacher ridiculed me in front of the whole class. He made me feel like a nobody and that I was stupid. That scene is branded in my brain forever. I can't forget it and I can never forgive him."

It is easy to sit in church or Sunday school and talk about forgiving other people. But it is not easy to do, is it? Ask the Jews who survived the Holocaust about forgiving the Germans who imprisoned them. Ask the citizens of Kuwait who survived the devastation in their country by Iraq. Ask the black South Africans who were victims of apartheid. Ask the Kurds who were displaced in their own countries. Ask some of the family members of those who died in the Twin Towers in New York City when planes crashed into them. Ask the young person who was raped on the college campus. Ask the man who was shot in the convenience store by a robber. Ask the teenager who is the victim of prejudice at school. Ask the child who is abused.

It is easy to talk about forgiveness until you have experienced some awful atrocity and are asked to forgive. When it happens to you, there is often no conversation about forgiveness. There is the demand for justice and that these people get what's coming to them. They need to be punished. All the conversation we have in church about forgiving other people seems downright silly when you are the one who's been hurt.

Forgiveness Wasn't Easy in Jesus' Day Either

But if we think it is difficult to forgive people today, can you imagine what it must have been like two thousand years ago when Jesus first spoke these words? His time was charged with political tyranny, slavery, cruelty, complete subjugation of women to men, and all the other difficulties and burdens that were a part of his ancient society. Yet Jesus spoke about the necessity of forgiving our brothers and sisters when they have wronged us. These words about forgiving were hard from the time they were first uttered.

How Many Times Do We Forgive?

We begin our examination of the text with Peter's question that attempts to put a limitation on forgiveness. Peter wanted to set up a yardstick to measure how many times it was necessary to forgive. He suggested seven times. In fact, he was thinking that his answer would please his Lord. After all, what he suggested was much better than most of the rabbis of his day suggested. They said people ought to forgive at least three times. Peter more than doubled that figure! "Lord, should we forgive seven times when somebody has done us wrong?" He thought he was quite pious. He was shining up his halo and waiting to be praised. But Jesus said to him, "No, Peter. You have to forgive seventy times seven." Jesus did not mean forgiveness is limited to four hundred and ninety times. That wasn't the point! Our forgiveness of another has to be unlimited. That is the point. We have to keep on forgiving. Peter asked the wrong question, because forgiveness is rooted in a person's attitude.

The Parable of the Debtor

To drive his point home, Jesus told a dramatic parable about a man with a debt beyond belief, an immeasurable debt. In the story, a servant of a king is called in for a reckoning, a day of judgment, with his master. We don't know what kind of servant he is, but to have spent this kind of money he must at least be a governor or some other person with considerable power and influence. The servant "was brought unto him," the text says. This likely indicates that the servant is already in prison. He is brought in before the king to be judged. According to the laws of Rome, if a man didn't have enough money to settle his debts he could be sold into slavery, along with family and everything he had. That is what the servant's master plans to do because of this debt. The servant's day of judgment has come.

Jesus uses an interesting figure to depict the size of this man's debt. Since we don't know much about the value of talents today, we often have difficulty sensing the enormous size of this debt. The text states that the man owed ten thousand talents. To get this debt in perspective, we have to understand that King Herod's annual revenue was about eight hundred talents. The servant's debt was greater than the taxes collected in all the provinces of Palestine. For one hundred talents, a hundred thousand men could be hired to fight one's battles for a year. An English scholar speculated that if this debt had to be paid in sixpence, the money would need to be carried by eight hundred and sixty men, each holding a sack weighing sixty pounds. If they walked a yard apart, they would form a line that stretched five miles. The man who owed one hundred denarii, by contrast, could put his coins in his pocket.

The debt this servant owes is enormous. Jesus is stating that it is an amount greater than the revenue of the man's own country. When the servant says, "Master, be patient with me, and I'll pay you back," the listeners who first heard this story would have broken into laughter. The absurdity of his claiming to pay back such a debt would have struck them as hilarious. Jesus gives such an exaggerated figure for the debt to reinforce the impossibility of anyone thinking he or she could pay it off. Trying to pay off this debt would be like a transient on the street being arrested and saying, "Oh, don't arrest me. I am going to pay for the national debt if you will just give me a little more time." It's a comical claim. The debt of the man in Jesus' story is beyond anybody's ability to pay. No individual, not *even* a king, could pay it.

Although this parable is not an allegory, if the king represents God—and in a way, I think he might—then Jesus is reminding us that our indebtedness to God is always immeasurable. Our debt to God is beyond anything we can ever repay. Like the servant in this parable, none of us can pay God back what we owe God. Our debt is too great. We have abused God's creation. We have in some way or another abused our relationships with other people. The psalmist has asked, "If you, LORD, should mark iniquities, O God, who shall stand?" (Ps 130:3). How can we repay God for our gossip, our wandering thoughts, our misuse of time, our mistreatment of nature, our harm to our own bodies, and the hurt we have caused others? How can we possibly measure our debt to God?

The Costly Nature of Sin

Look at the awful cost of our sinfulness. It is sad how often people try to act as though sin is nothing. Many wink at sin. Or they oversimplify forgiveness and miss it by saying, "Just say, 'I'm sorry,' and everything will be all right!" This parable drives home the point that sin is not cheap. Jesus reminds us that sin is harsh and devastating in its effects on God. The cost of the damage to the heart of God is immeasurable and beyond our ability to repay. Too many of us are like the atheist who lay dying on his bed. Somebody asked him if he was afraid of dying. "Oh, no. It's God's business to forgive." For people who take this attitude, it doesn't make any difference what they do. They assume God will forgive them no matter what. But we do not read the Scriptures well when we have that attitude.

The servant in Jesus' parable can never pay his unbelievably large and insurmountable debt, but he falls on his knees and begs his master to be patient with him, promising to repay it. What he receives is unbelievable generosity. He receives a gift from his master. His master wipes all of his debt off the slate and sets the servant free. This is unbelievable and undeserved grace!

A church member told me some time ago that she had borrowed five thousand dollars from a nephew to do some remodeling work at her home. She used the money to build a spare room. When she requested the loan, she told her nephew, "I want to borrow this money. I don't expect you to give it to me. I am going to pay you back a little every month." So she did. She paid him fifty dollars a month for several months. On her birthday, she received a card from her nephew. "My wife and I have recently been very fortunate and have come into a little bit of money," her nephew wrote, "and I want to tell you that your debt is forgiven. You no longer owe us anything." She said that she was so elated she didn't know what to do. She addressed a letter to her nephew and his wife. She didn't write a thing on the first page, but on the back of the paper, she wrote, "I don't know what to say, I don't know what to say, I don't know what to say. Thank you!" Then she signed her name. A new family had just moved next door to her. She cranked up her lawn mower and began to cut their grass. The new neighbor came out and asked, "What are you doing? Who are you?" She had not even met them! She introduced herself and told them her story. Then she said, "I just wanted to do something to help somebody else because of what has been done for me." Her debt was wiped clean. She received generosity from another person. This is what happened to the servant in Jesus' parable.

Forgiving in the Real World

But the scene in Jesus' parable changes. "The same servant went out." He walked out the door. He went out from the presence of his master into the rugged walks of life. It is easy when we are sitting in church to look pious in our Sunday finery. We sing hymns, pray, be silent, and half listen to the preacher. But then we have to leave and go out into the world. In the world, we have to live out our Christian faith, and it gets tough. Sometimes we are ridiculed or people make fun of us. Sometimes people say, "I can't really do what I should as a Christian because it is a tough world out there. It is a dog-eat-dog world. You can't do what you used to be able to do. You have to play hardball. You've got to watch out for number one. It is hard to be a Christian in the world."

How can we forgive other people? What would our country be like if we simply wiped out the debts everyone owed? What would our world be like if folks didn't pay their debts? We know: honest folks would have to pay them. "That's the reason we have bill collectors," someone may quip. Many Christians feel that they have to leave all their Christian values inside the church when they go into the world. That is what the servant in our parable does.

Unwilling to Forgive

When the servant goes out from his master's presence where he has just been forgiven an immeasurable debt, he meets a servant of his own, someone under his employment who owes him about twenty dollars. When he sees the servant, he grabs him by the throat, reflecting violent feelings, and demands, "Pay what you owe." This man's servant falls on his knees, just like the man did earlier before his master, and begs for patience so that he will have time to pay his debt. But no, the servant uses a different standard for this man than the king applied to himself. He sets a higher standard for others than for himself. He has higher expectations of other people than of himself. He was forgiven, but he will not forgive others. He has received, but he will not give.

Don't think that such an attitude is confined to the servant in this story. If we look in the mirror, we discover that it is easier to criticize other people than to take criticism. It is easier to be rude than to be the victim of rudeness. It is easier to curse somebody else than to be cursed. Sometimes it is easier to expect more of other people than we do of ourselves. We can excuse our own behavior by saying, "I just didn't feel good today," or "I am sleepy," or "I am tired." We easily excuse our own actions. Our expectations are greater for others than they are for ourselves.

Lack of Gratitude

Notice also that this man seems ungrateful for the forgiveness he has just received. For some, it seems easier to receive forgiveness than it is to give it. The servant in Jesus' story sees himself as an exception to the rules. But before we condemn him, let's remember how much we are like him. Think about the hard feelings you harbor toward someone who has hurt you sometime in your life—maybe a parent, a child, a friend, a husband, wife, or some other relative. Somebody may have said something to hurt your feelings. Their words continue to burn in your mind, and you can't let them go. You harbor bitter feelings, cling to some slight remark, some trivial offense, and hang on to the words of criticism until they begin to fester within you. You won't let them go. I have known people who don't come to church anymore because of something somebody said or didn't say twenty-five years ago. There are people in our churches who won't speak to each other because of something one did or said to the other. Think of what this attitude does to them emotionally.

In the comic strip *Andy Capp*, which is told in an English setting, Andy spends a lot of time at the pub. Andy is always trying to dodge his pastor or vicar, and usually his wife Flo comes to the rescue. One day Flo rescues Andy from the pub once again and leads him home. Andy is obviously a bit inebriated. "I'm so glad you took him back again," the vicar says. "There's something about me," Flo replies. "I just have to forgive and forget." But behind his hand, Andy comments as Flo is pulling him along, "There's something about her, all right. She never forgets that she forgives." Some of us cling to whatever another person has done to us and we harbor it within our spirits. Later we throw it into their faces and are not willing to let them forget it. This kind of attitude destroys relationships and destroys us. We become victims of our own hatred.

The Result of Refusing to Forgive

In verse 35, we find the most difficult saying in this passage: "And so angry was the master that he condemned the man to torture until he should pay the debt in full. That is how my heavenly Father will deal with you, unless you each forgive your brother (or sister) from your heart." The point is that when we refuse to forgive other people, we close our own hearts to God. We cut ourselves off from our relationship to God. We say we only need to repent to be forgiven by God. But repentance cannot take place if we have closed our hearts to forgiving other people. Jesus taught us to pray, "Forgive us our trespasses as we forgive those who have trespassed against us." Our willingness to forgive others unlocks the door, opens the fountain, so God's grace can come into our lives. When we refuse to forgive, hold grudges, or harbor hatred toward other people, God's grace cannot touch us. We poison ourselves. Our souls become dyed the color of our thoughts of bitterness, hatred, anxiety, and criticism. When someone says, "I'll never forgive," he or she is cut off from sensing God's forgiveness.

I know it is not easy to forgive some people. I know it is not easy to forgive perpetrators of abuse. It is not easy to forgive bearers of hatred or gossip. Yet, if we are unwilling to forgive those who have wronged us, we cut ourselves off from God's forgiveness. If we are unwilling to forgive another person, we destroy the bridge that grace passes over.

Bill Jones was a marvelous preacher and pastor at Bethany Baptist Church in Brooklyn, New York. One of his parishioners went out of the church one Sunday, and when Dr. Jones asked her how she was, she said, "Well, pastor, I'll tell you. I'm somewhere between 'Thank you, Jesus,' and 'Lord, have mercy.'" That is likely where all of us are in the struggle to forgive others. We want to thank God for what we have already accomplished in overcoming our sins, but we also want to say, "Lord, have mercy; we know we have so far to go yet." We have to learn to relate to those with whom we differ, who have different opinions, attitudes, philosophies, tastes, customs, and ideas than our own. We may be hurt, misunderstood, or criticized. If we are unwilling to forgive others, we not only harm our relationships with them but also harm ourselves and our relationship with God.

The Desire to Restore Relationships

Jesus is *not* in the business of trying to punish or destroy people. He wants to redeem people. If you and I are going to follow our Lord when people have hurt us, our response should not be to see if we can hurt them or do harm to them. It should be to find out how we can restore the relationship and bring redemption, wholeness, fullness, and completeness into their lives and our own.

In the midst of the Civil War, Abraham Lincoln made a complimentary comment about the Southern states, and a woman who heard it was outraged. She could not understand how he could speak kindly of his enemies when he should want to crush them. Looking at her, Lincoln said quietly, "Madam, do I not destroy my enemies when I make them my friends?" When we learn to be brothers and sisters to each other, we are no longer enemies. We seek not to hurt each other but to love and build up the body of Christ, his church.

Actions to Take

What can you do? Some of you know what you need to do. You need to apologize to somebody you have hurt. You need to say, "I am sorry." You may need to do this in person, make a phone call, or write a letter or text. Your problem with an unwillingness to forgive may be so severe that some of you need professional counseling. Seek that. Talk to a minister or a trained counselor. Learn to forgive others so your hatred doesn't destroy you. Forgive others so you can fulfill God's purpose for you and sense God's grace in a greater capacity.

A church was engaged in renewal and revival services some years ago. One night, when the invitation was given, two men came from opposite sides of the church and knelt at the altar. They had been bitter enemies for years. Neither one knew that the other had come forward. When they stood up, each had just made a new commitment to God, and they saw each other for the first time. They had not spoken for years. Suddenly they embraced one another and asked for forgiveness. This is what Jesus is telling us to do. God has forgiven all of us of an unbelievable debt of sin, and he says to us, "Look at the small debt this person has that you need to forgive. Listen and act today."

Listen to the words of our Lord in the sixth chapter of Matthew:

> "When you pray, say 'forgive us the wrongs we have done, as we have forgiven those who have wronged us.' For if you forgive others the wrongs they have done, your heavenly Father will also forgive you, but if you do not forgive others, then the wrongs you have done will not be forgiven by your Father." (Matt 6:12, 14-15)

Open the door of forgiveness in your own heart, so that you too can experience the wideness of God's wonderful grace.

8

If God Already Knows, Why Should I Pray?

Matthew 6:5-8

Like many pastors, I am occasionally invited, along with my wife, into the home of a church member for a meal. It is interesting to observe the behavior of the family when we sit at the table and some of the children begin eating immediately. The hostess reminds her children abruptly, "We haven't said the blessing yet." She then calls upon the pastor to return thanks for the food. After the prayer is said and I butter my roll, she says, "Well, now, Pastor, you have to understand we do not always say grace at our meals here." I want to say that is obvious. But in silence I continue to butter my roll, because I know what line is coming next. "We simply assume that the Lord knows we are thankful for what we're getting," she continues, "and we don't think we have to remind him all the time."

The Context of this Passage

The Scripture passage in Matthew 6:5-8 is one that these people might use as their proof-text for such a thought. After all, if the Lord already knows what we need, why bother to tell God anything? Let's see if we can discern the meaning of this Scripture. It is set within an interesting context. Jesus has just finished denouncing hypocritical prayer. The tradition of Judaism prescribed prayers three times a day. When the time for daily prayers arrived, many of the Pharisees, rather than being in a secluded, private place, would select a conspicuous street corner to pray. In that spot, or in the synagogue, they would pray loudly and fervently unto the Lord. They could be seen by all those who passed by or attended the synagogue. Jesus said this ostentatious display was for the purpose of receiving praise from their fellow men and women. They wanted the approval of others. Jesus said that approval, indeed, was the only reward they would receive in answer to such prayers. Instead of a public display, Jesus encourages his followers to go into a secret chamber when they pray, to close and lock the door behind them so that God alone hears and sees the prayer. Our prayers are not for notice and praise but to commune with God.

Endless Prayer Repetitions

Next, Jesus refers to the endless babble of some pagans in their prayers toward God. In some pagan traditions, various phrases were utilized to present an almost endless list of the names of God, sometimes in the thousands, in hopes that somehow the one praying might possibly say the correct name for God. This endless repetition of phrases and meaningless words was often used in an attempt to browbeat God or weary God into responding to their requests. They thought God might get tired of hearing their repetitions and give in to them. They believed if they just prayed hard enough or long enough, they might persuade or coerce God into granting their wishes. But even in our Christian traditions, we sometimes follow that practice. Our use of "Now I lay me down to sleep" for children's bedtime prayers or our repetition of the Lord's Prayer may become a farce as they are parroted without us thinking about the meaning of our words.

Inadequate Prayers

Having warned people about the problem of using prayer as a sham before God, Jesus declares, "You need to know that your Father already knows what you are going to ask before you ask it." Many of us want to exclaim, "Wait a minute, Jesus. You taught us on another occasion, 'Whatever you ask for in prayer, believe that you will receive it, and it will be yours'" (Mark 11:24). Jesus urges us to ask, knock, and seek in our prayers. "I don't understand, Jesus," we might say. "Your words in Matthew 6:5-8 seem to contradict what you have said elsewhere."

There is no question that a lot of people use prayer primarily as a means to ask for certain "things." They pray, "Lord, give me this and give me that." Their prayers are filled with "give me." Prayer is turned into a magic talisman. When the Catholic nuns and priests were expelled from

Cuba in 1961, one story emerged about Communists who discredited religion by degrading prayer. The Communists would line up small children in school and then instruct them, "We want you to pray to God for some candy or a toy and then hold out your hands to receive it." The children would then pray for a toy or candy. "Look into your hands," the Communists would instruct. "Did you receive anything?" "No," said the children. "Well, pray harder. Pray louder. Ask God again to give you toys or candy." They, of course, received no candy or toys. Then the Communists would say, "Let us try something else. We have a new government. It is one that will educate you and give your fathers jobs so they can buy you candy and toys. Now ask your new leader, Premier Castro, to give you a toy or candy. Hold out your hand." They were given a toy or candy as they desired. "See," the Communists declared, "this shows there is no God. Your new redeemer is Fidel Castro."

Asking in Christ's Name

When our prayers are reduced to the level of simply asking or begging for something, they often go unanswered. But we overlook the words from our Lord that establish the condition in our prayers: "if you *abide in me* and if you ask *in my name*." "Abiding in Christ" and "asking in his name" do not give us permission to ask for all kinds of selfish materialistic things. A prayer in the name of Christ is spoken by someone who seeks to be in the will of Christ and has the desire to do what God wants for the world. To pray in Jesus' name is to live under the guidance and control of God. It is to live with God at our elbow. This kind of prayer rejects selfish concerns for the higher concerns of Christ. To pray "in Christ's name" puts our prayer in a whole new dimension.

God Knows All Things

If we pray and God already knows our needs, why should we ask at all? Some say, "It is God's business to forgive, so why should I ask?" These people assume that God knows what they need and that he will meet that need. But that is a naive way of perceiving God. We could approach this subject another way. Frederick Speakman, in a sermon titled "Does God Read His Children's Mail?" raised the question, "What if God doesn't respond unless he's told or shown?" His thesis was that God doesn't read our mail. If we don't ask him, he won't respond. This is one of the limits that God has set upon himself. Without our asking, he will not react. We need to ask if he is going to respond. "What if that's one of the rules of God's game,"

Speakman proposed, "that He will not eavesdrop at the keyhole of our souls unless there's some indication of welcome, that He will not slip in to read our minds unless some signal is given?"[1]

There is no question God has given us freedom of will; we have the ability to reject him and run away from him. But I am not convinced that Speakman presents a clear picture of God's nature. There are surely some things that God will do for us, I believe, even if we do not ask. But that is not true of all things. And surely God knows what we do and think, whether or not we are willing to acknowledge God in our own thoughts or behavior. We may not be able to receive God's grace because we refuse to accept it, but that doesn't prohibit God's knowledge of our needs and faults. We are indeed given the freedom to respond or not to respond, but that doesn't lessen God's awareness of the situation. This passage from Jesus implies that God knows all matters.

How We Should Pray

Note this truth about our text: when Jesus says that our Father already knows what we need before we ask it, he doesn't add, "Therefore don't pray." Look at the verse again. "Your Father knows what your needs are before you ask him." But then Jesus continues, "This is how you should pray." He proceeds to give them an example of how they should pray in the model prayer. Just because the Father knows our needs is not a reason to avoid praying. We should pray. Jesus himself is an example of the importance of prayer. His whole life was a testimony to the need for constant prayer. Jesus prayed at his baptism, while he was in the wilderness, before he chose his disciples, before he fed the multitude with the loaves and fish, before he raised Lazarus from the dead, and on a mountaintop where he was transfigured. Sometimes Jesus prayed all night long. He prayed in the upper room, on the Mount of Olives before he was arrested, and while hanging on the cross in agony and dying. The last thing we see Jesus do is pray. His life was surrounded with prayer. Just because God knows our needs is no excuse not to pray.

But listen carefully to Jesus' words here: "Your Father knows what your needs are." Our needs are often very different from what we want or wish. We have all kinds of wants, wishes, desires, and whims. A number of years ago, the pastor of a small church was attending seminary. He said that he prayed for God to give him a Cadillac, and God gave it to him. What he actually did was convince some of his deacons to pay for the car and think that action was doing God's will. This selfish, magical concept is not what

Jesus means by God responding to our needs. God doesn't grant our every want and wish. God responds according to our needs, and that is radically different from our wants or secret desires. A responsible parent or teacher or pastor does not always give his or her children, students, or parishioners what they want. The goal is to give them what they need. A parent, teacher, or pastor wants to give people what will enable them to grow and become mature. Our wants, wishes, and desires may not be for our best overall good. God seeks to give us what is best for us to meet the deepest needs in our lives. God does not have to be persuaded to do this; he is already concerned about our best interests.

The prayer of an unknown Confederate soldier is set in bronze in the lobby of the Institute of Physical Medicine and Rehabilitation in New York City. Take these words to heart:

> I asked God for strength, that I might do greater things,
> I was made weak, that I might learn humbly to obey . . .
> I asked for health, that I might do greater things,
> I was given infirmity, that I might do better things . . .
> I asked for riches, that I might be happy,
> I was given poverty, that I might be wise . . .
> I asked for power, that I might have the praise of men,
> I was given weakness, that I might feel the need of God . . .
> I asked for all things, that I might enjoy life,
> I was given life, that I might enjoy all things . . .
> I got nothing that I asked for—but everything I had hoped for,
> Almost despite myself, my unspoken prayers were answered,
> I am among all men, most richly blessed.

God Responds to Our Needs

We should be thankful that God does not grant our prayers merely according to our wants. Instead, God responds to our needs. He answers us in ways that will enable us to grow. C. S. Lewis has said it well: "We can bear to be refused [by God] but not to be ignored. In other words, our faith can survive many refusals if they really are refusals and not disregards."[2] We all want to believe that God hears our prayers and responds, even if his response is "No." Deep down, we know we can accept a "no," but we could not accept it if God did not care. Why pray then if God already knows our needs? We pray because prayer is the vehicle that opens us to God's grace. It's the medium through which we grow in that grace. It's where our deepest needs are met.

Have you ever noticed how values sometimes get twisted around? The older I get the more I am amazed at how values in our society seem completely distorted, turned upside down. This distortion of values is like going into a store and finding priceless diamonds selling for nickels and dimes while cheap trinkets are selling for thousands of dollars. For example, we pay entertainers and athletes millions of dollars but pay those who teach our children wages that sometimes border on the poverty level. What does that say about us as a society? What does it reveal about our values as a nation when our entertainers and athletes are paid more than the people who teach our children? Follow this thought into the dimension of prayer. As Christians, we claim that spiritual matters are the most important values in our lives. Yet we give little attention to developing our spiritual lives. We spend most of our efforts and strength to acquire material things. Rather than seeking spiritual growth, our ultimate goal seems to be to acquire more and more material things and to be better and better entertained. We do almost nothing to develop the inner life.

Why Pray?

If God already knows our deepest needs, why should we pray? We pray to open the doors of our hearts to the eternal God and prepare ourselves for eternity. All the material things we acquire in this life will come to an end soon, and if we have done nothing to prepare our inner selves, what will we take with us into eternity?

If God already knows our needs, why should we pray? Prayer is a doorway to worship God. Prayer is a means for us to lift up our voices in praise and adoration to God. Psalm 42:1 reminds us, "As the deer longs for the flowing streams, my heart longs for God." Prayer is a medium through which we might learn to love God with all our hearts, souls, mind, and strength, and to love our neighbors as we love ourselves. We pray not so much for what we can get from praying but as a way to do something for God. We pray to praise God, to adore God, and to sense God's presence.

If God already knows what our needs are, why should we pray? We pray so we can confess our sins. As we come into God's holy presence, we are aware of our weaknesses and inadequacies. God's holiness reveals our limitations and emptiness. Before God, we confess our fragmented nature and how frail and fragile we are. We acknowledge that our sin is ever before us (Ps 51). In the presence of the holiness of God, we declare our need of God. We confess our insufficiency. Through rigorous self-examination, with all alibis removed, we seek to be open to God's cleansing love, to let

God's light and fresh air into our lives. In prayer, we freely confess our weaknesses and need of God. Our needs often drive us to prayer.

I sometimes talk with people who have confessed their sins. I ask them to write these sins on a piece of paper. After praying for forgiveness, I ask them to tear the paper into small pieces. In some retreat settings, they have dropped these pieces of paper into a flowing stream and let the water bear them away. Or they have torn up the pieces of paper on which they wrote their sins and dropped them into an open fire. This symbolized the removal and cleansing of their sins. With the psalmist, they could now affirm that "as far as the east is from the west, God has removed our sins from us" (Ps 103:12). Prayer can enable us to experience the wonderful grace and forgiveness of God. We pray to experience the forgiving love of God.

If God already knows our needs, why pray? We pray so that we might have a sense of God's presence and be able to commune with God. Prayer is a relationship. It is personal communion, fellowship, engagement with the holy Other—God. We open the door of our souls to invite God into the deepest regions of our spirits. In a world where we are constantly bombarded with so much noise that tries to guide what we want, which way we should go, where we should sleep, eat, or travel, we come before God in silence. We can go apart in a particular place, at a particular time, and be still and silent so we can listen for the sound of the gentle stillness of God's presence. We do this to close out the noise of the world and go inward to develop our lives. We must strive to practice the presence of God.

Prayer Opens Our Lives to God

In the stillness, we wait. We wait to sense God's Spirit coming into our lives. We open our lives to be nurtured by God. In that silence, quietness, and "apart-ness," we wait like parched soil for rain to nourish it. We wait like tiny baby birds in a nest with their mouths open to the food that the mother or father bird will bring. We wait like sand on a beach for the ocean waves to break upon us. We wait like the cold earth in winter as the snow falls. We wait like a tiny baby on his or her mother's breast, longing to be fed. We wait like a flower reaching up to feel the warmth of the sun on a spring morning. In silence, we wait to be fed by God and to be nurtured by him. That is why we pray.

Sometimes words are unnecessary, insufficient, and inadequate. I encourage you simply to wait before God. Sometimes our words may get in the way of praying. If we want to focus on God and do what some spiritualists call "centering," maybe a few phrases will be helpful to bring our wandering minds back: simple phrases like "Jesus is Lord," "Lord, have mercy," "Lord, it's me, and I need you today," or "The Lord is my shepherd." Use simple phrases to focus your mind on God. Keep words to a minimum. You might pray quietly, "O Lord, you know my needs. I wait for you to respond." The Scriptures tell us that the Spirit of God is within us. Our deepest needs may never rise to our lips, but God knows these needs, and his Spirit, through groans and aches within us, expresses these needs to God. God knows these deep needs.

I do think it is important to acknowledge our needs and express them to God when we know what they are. We then wait in silence for God to nurture and feed us. We empty our lives to be filled by God. P. T. Forsyth has reminded us that prayer "is the central act of the soul . . . . To be religious is to pray. Bad prayer is false religion. Not to pray is to be irreligious . . . . In prayer, we do not think God out; we draw him out. Prayer is where our thought of God passes into action, and becomes more certain than thought."[3] If we never pray, how do we expect to commune with God? Prayer is the way to commune and meditate with the Eternal.

Praying as Commitment of Our Lives to God

If God already knows what our needs are, why pray? Praying gives us a chance to commit or recommit our lives more deeply to God. The Westminster Shorter Catechism gives a good definition of prayer. It reads, "Prayer is an offering up of our desires unto God, for things agreeable to his will, in the name of Christ, with confession of our sins, and thankful acknowledgment of his mercies." We pray because we want to be in God's will. We seek to give ourselves without reserve to God. We should not pray to try to change God's mind and twist God's will to our will. We should not pray to see if we can use enough words to make God tired and weary and give in to our wishes out of fatigue. Instead, we should pray to discover what God wants for our lives in order that we may live according to what God wants for us. We should always pray, "Lord this may be what I want, but I know it may not be what I need. Your will be done. Your will be done." God's will is not always what I want, but it will always be what I need. God doesn't have to be asked to respond, but he does want us to acknowledge our own needs. It is not so much that God needs to be asked as that we have a need to ask God. The burden is with us, not God.

Rowan Williams, former archbishop of Canterbury and master at Magdalene College at Cambridge University, draws on insights from Origen, the Alexandrian theologian of the middle third century who wrote a little book that was the first systematic study of prayer. Origen raised the question, "If God knows what we are going to ask, why bother to pray?" Williams believes that Origen gave as good an answer as anyone could give. He summarizes Origen's response in these words:

> God knows, of course, what we are going to say and do, but God has decided that he will work out his purposes through what we decide to say and do. So if it is God's will to bring something about, some act of healing or reconciliation, some change for the better in the world, he has chosen that your prayer is going to be a part of a set of causes that make it happen. So you'd better get on with it, as you and your prayer are a part of God's overall purpose for the situation in which he is going to work.[4]

We pray with the goal of seeking to link our lives with God's purpose and will, and then we strive to labor with and for God to bring about God's divine purpose. As we pray, we acknowledge that God will neither do for us what we can do ourselves nor always respond or guide us in the way we may assume is best.

One of the foremost theologians during the Second World War was Dietrich Bonhoeffer. Bonhoeffer came to America for a visit when the war broke out. Some of his friends at Union Theological Seminary, like Reinhold Niebuhr, tried to persuade him to stay in the States so he could be safe. Bonhoeffer would not do that. He wanted to go back to Germany and be with his people. But he could not listen to Hitler's words without speaking out against them.

After Bonhoeffer denounced Hitler's practices, he was arrested and put in a Nazi concentration camp. While he was a prisoner, this theologian's devotional life was so contagious that it affected everybody in that concentration camp—both the inmates and the Nazi soldiers. His daily devotions in the Nazi prison camp not only helped him personally but deeply inspired all the people in the camp. A Nazi prison doctor wrote these words: "Through the half-open door of a room in one of the huts I saw Pastor Bonhoeffer, still in his prison clothes, kneeling in fervent prayer to the Lord his God. The devotion and evident conviction of being heard that I saw in the prayer of this intensive captivating man moved me to the depths."

Bonhoeffer prayed for many things, I am sure. In his letters home, he wrote that he hoped to rejoin his family and teach again. But that prayer was not granted. He was taken out one day to be hanged. In his biography by Mary Bosanquet, she gives us this picture of him: "Naked under the scaffold in the sweet spring woods, Bonhoeffer knelt for the last time to pray. Five minutes later his life was ended."[5] He had whispered to a friend just a short while before that, "For me this is the not end, but the beginning." Bonhoeffer, like all of us, had prayed that he might be set free and go home. But that prayer was not answered. I do not know why. But I do know this: when Bonhoeffer had to face his death, his faith sustained him. Why? He had already given his life in daily communion with God. In the moment of dying, he knew that nothing could separate him from God.

Why should we pray if God already knows our needs? We pray so we can have such a relationship with God that no matter what enters our lives, whether it is tribulation, distress, persecution, famine, nakedness, illness, peril, or death, we know that we will never be separated from God when we are in Christ Jesus. Let's build that relationship. Open our lives to God. Be nurtured by God. Strengthen our spiritual lives through daily prayer. Let's pray that we will seek to grow more deeply in our knowledge of God.[6]

The *Pilgrim's Hymn* by Stephen Paulus affirms our deepest prayers:

> Even before we call on Your name
> To ask You, O God,
> When we seek for the words to glorify You,
> You hear our prayer;
> Unceasing love, O unceasing love,
> Surpassing all we know.
>
> Glory to the Father, and to the Son,
> And to the Holy Spirit.
>
> Even with darkness sealing us in,
> We breathe Your name,
> And through all the days that follow so fast,
> We trust in You;
> Endless Your grace, O endless Your grace,
> Beyond all mortal dream.
>
> Both now and forever,
> And unto ages and ages,
> Amen.[7]

Notes

1. Frederick Speakman, *Love Is Something You Do* (Westwood NJ: Fleming H. Revell Co., 1969) 119.

2. C. S. Lewis, *Prayer: Letters to Malcolm* (Glasgow: William Collins Sons, & Co., 1964) 55.

3. P. T. Forsyth, *The Soul of Prayer* (Grand Rapids MI: Wm. B. Eerdmans Publishing Co., 1916) 19.

4. Rowan Williams, *Being Christian: Baptism, Eucharist, Prayer* (Grand Rapids MI: Eerdmans, 2014), excerpted in *The Christian Century* (6 August 2014): 20–21.

5. Mary Bosanquet, *The Life and Death of Dietrich Bonhoeffer* (New York: Harper & Row, 1968) 278.

6. For further study on praying in difficult times, see my book, William Powell Tuck, *Lord, I Keep Getting a Busy Signal: Reaching for a Better Spiritual Connection* (Gonzalez FL: Energion Publications, 2014).

7. Stephen Paulus, "The Pilgrim's Hymn," musicanet.org/en/texts/00/00059en.htm.

9

Jesus' Teaching on Divorce

Matthew 5:31-32; Mark 10:1-12

The institution of marriage is being accosted on many fronts today. Some are saying marriage is obsolete. Others declare that to get married is sheer lunacy. Others are choosing not to get married at all but simply to live together without formal marriage.

In the United States, one divorce occurs every thirteen seconds, which makes our country sixth on a global scale. Divorce is most common in the first four or five years of marriage. The mental health and educational level of the couple affects the possibility of divorce as well. Divorce continues to be a serious problem in the United States today.[1]

Researchers have found that the claim that half of marriages end in divorce is not true. In fact, divorce rates have fallen in recent years. Studies have shown that the divorce rate in the United States peaked at about 40 percent around 1980 and has been declining ever since. Data from the *National Survey of Family Growth* found that there was a 65 percent probability of a first marriage for women lasting for a decade and 70 percent for men. Other statistics reveal that three-quarters of those married in the 1990s would remain married fifteen years compared to 65 percent of those married in the 1980s.[2] Statistics also show that those who marry before age twenty-five tend to divorce earlier. The best age for marrying, according to these studies, seems to be between twenty-eight and thirty-two. Additionally, those with a college degree are less likely to divorce.[3] While these more recent statistics are encouraging, they are still high.

Divorce Is Not New

Divorce is not new in society. Unfortunately, it has a long history. In the ancient Jewish world, marriage was considered sacred. It was a man's duty to get married and have children so that the race could be perpetuated. But a woman was considered part of a man's property. She had few rights. The husband could divorce his wife with a piece of paper, but she could not divorce him unless he was willing to give her a divorce.

In the Greek world in the time of Jesus, a wife was seen primarily as a person to bear a man's children. A man sought pleasure through other means. The wife was supposed to remain chaste, but the husband was free to fulfill his desires wherever he wished. In the Roman world, marriage was considered sacred for generations. Soon after the Roman army conquered the Greeks, the Greeks began to influence Rome. Marriages began to deteriorate within the Roman Empire as they had in Greece. But the Romans did grant women the right to get a divorce.

Jesus Is Tested

The Gospels of Matthew, Mark, and Luke tell about an experience Jesus had when some Pharisee lawyers questioned him. It was a trick question. "Moses gave a bill of divorcement," they said to Jesus. "We want to know if you think there are grounds for divorce." At the time, there were two schools of thought about divorce among the Jews. The interpretations were based on Deuteronomy 24:1. One school was the Shammai, which taught that there was only one reason for divorce: unchastity or, as sometimes translated, adultery.

The Hillel school held to a more liberal interpretation of Deuteronomy 24:1. Their interpretation of the Hebrew words for "some uncleanness" might refer to a number of things a woman might do. The matter might be a trivial thing like putting too much salt in her husband's food or speaking to a man on the street or making disrespectful remarks about her husband's father in his presence. The husband often divorced his wife for trivial reasons.

The Pharisees raised the question about divorce in the hopes of entrapping Jesus. They knew that no matter where he landed in this Jewish argument, he would anger somebody. They were also aware that Herodias, a granddaughter of Herod the Great, had been married to her uncle Herod Philip. But she became infatuated with another uncle, Herod Antipas, and so she divorced Philip to marry the other uncle. Although Jewish law did not give her the power to get a divorce, she was a Roman citizen, and Rome did give women that legal right. Herodias was the woman whom John the Baptist condemned for living in adultery. He was beheaded for this bold accusation. The Pharisees believed that if they could get Jesus to make an accusatory statement about divorce, they could offend one of the schools of the Pharisees and maybe even get Jesus in trouble with the Roman government. "What do you say, Jesus?" they asked.

The Oldest Version of the Story

Listen to the oldest version of this story as recorded in Mark 10:1-12:

> On leaving those parts Jesus came into a region of Judaea in TransJordan; and when a crowd gathered around him once again, he followed his usual practice and taught them. The question was put to him: "Is it lawful for a man to divorce his wife?" This was to test him. He asked in return, "What did Moses command you?" They answered, "Moses permitted a man to divorce his wife by note of dismissal." Jesus said to them, "It was because your minds were closed that he made this rule for you; but in the beginning, at the creation, God made them male and female. For this reason, a man shall leave his father and mother, and be made one with his wife; and the two shall become one flesh. It follows that they are no longer two individuals; they are one flesh. What God has joined together, man must not separate." When they were indoors again the disciples questioned him about this matter; he said to them, "Whoever divorces his wife and marries another commits adultery against her: so too, if she divorces her husband and marries another, she commits adultery."

These were hard words then and they are hard words today. No wonder most preachers avoid speaking on them. I would rather avoid them too, except for the fact that this passage has always troubled me, and I feel like I need to probe it for some answers. I know that my interpretation will not make everybody happy, and maybe I will make nobody happy. But I don't think it's wise to ignore the passage.

Look at the Except Clause

We must begin in recognition of a problem with our biblical texts. Matthew's Gospel presents an "except clause." Jesus says a man should not divorce a woman *except* for adultery. In Mark's Gospel, there is no "except clause" at all. This is one of the problems people have when they study the Scriptures. One passage we read may present the same story in a slightly different way. If we don't examine the biblical texts and compare them but simply take all of them literally, we will have a problem. Readers sometimes have to decide, by learning from biblical scholars, which parts of Scripture come from the oldest tradition and the most reliable biblical source.

For several reasons, almost all scholars are convinced that Mark's Gospel is the oldest and most accurate of the four Gospels. First, the parallel of Matthew 5:31-32 in Luke 16:18 also gives no "except clause." Second, when Paul writes about divorce in 1 Corinthians 7:10, he does not allow exceptions either, and his letter is likely older than Mark. Third, in the Mark text Jesus appeals to the creation account in Genesis and not to the law. Fourth, it seems clear from this context that Jesus is making an absolute demand. Finally, the fact that, in Matthew's account, Jesus' disciples are greatly disturbed by this teaching shows the harshness of the demand. They ask Jesus, "Lord, if this is true, should we really get married? Wouldn't it be more expedient to remain single?" (Matt 19:10). In agreement with most scholars, I think Mark's account is the original story. Matthew's Gospel was directed to Jewish readers, and it is likely that a Jewish editor inserted the traditional Jewish thought that divorce should be denied "except" on grounds of adultery. Now then, keeping in mind the oldest text of this story in Mark 10, what is Jesus teaching us about marriage and divorce?

The Ideal of Marriage

Jesus is holding before his listeners the ideal of marriage. His appeal is not to the law but to creation. He reaches behind the law and goes all the way back to creation when God created man and woman. Divorce, he says, is grounded in the law, but marriage is grounded in creation. When God created man and woman, God made them male and female. Jesus stated that Moses permitted a bill of divorce because of "your hardness of heart" (Mark 10:5). Having hardness of heart means being "closed-minded," "stubborn," or "un-teachable." In the Mark passage, Jesus is stating that Moses granted a bill of divorce as a concession to people's human weakness. But this was contrary to God's purpose in creation.

Jesus Championed the Cause of Women

In Mark's Gospel, Jesus, like he did on other occasions, championed the cause of women. Women often suffered injustices at the hands of their husbands. In the Jewish tradition, a woman could not ask for a divorce; only the man had that right. Jesus does not subordinate the woman to the man but notes that if either man or woman divorces, each has dishonored the permanency of marriage. Jesus declares that a woman, if she gets a divorce, is just as guilty as a man who divorces his wife.

The Roman government allowed both men and women the right to get a divorce. Jesus is stating that both parties in a marriage, likewise, need to keep their end of the covenant. Jesus lifts marriage out of the mire of the commonplace to a lofty plain of radical demand. Many find this demand frightening because it summons each person to a deeper commitment than what might be expected. This teaching from Jesus is certainly demanding, but it follows the other teachings he has given us.

Consider, for example, the way William Luck summarizes three of these teachings, with Jesus looking at the motive of a person's potential actions:[4]

1. In Matthew 5:21-25, Jesus states, "You think that you are innocent of murder, because you only did it in your heart? You are wrong. You are guilty of murder!"

2. In Matthew 5:27-29, he says, "You think you are innocent of adultery, because you have only lusted in your mind? You are wrong. You are guilty of adultery."

3. In Matthew 5:31-32, he says, "You think you are innocent of adultery, because you have a legal writ (a piece of paper). You are wrong. You are guilty of adultery!"

God's Intention from Creation

Jesus upholds an absolute ideal for all people that is based on God's original creation. The Jewish word for marriage means consecration. In their covenant together, a man and a woman consecrate themselves completely to each other. Each is exclusively the possession of the other as an offering that is exclusively dedicated to God. Each is so committed to the other that the two of them become one flesh. This union was God's act in creation, and any breaking of this union is the action of men and women, not God.

A permanent union was God's intention from creation. This union is more than a sexual bonding. It is a union in which each person strives to help develop the other's personality. Each seeks to enable the other person to become a full, total human being. Each seeks to contribute whatever makes the other a total person. We can never "complete" another person in our love for him or her, but our aim should be that our love and relationship should support and enable the other to be the best person he or she can be with our support and love. Each of us is certainly an authentic person in one's self, however, hopefully our marriage partner will enable him or her to find one's own potential and not hinder it.

Too many attribute love to an emotional sexuality. The question is, "Are you attracted physically to somebody?" Many call that love. But sex is only a tiny portion of real, genuine love. Love encompasses so much more than sex. Sex is a very important part of marriage, but it does not encompass all that is involved in love.

Do You Love Me?

In the musical *Fiddler on the Roof*, a dairyman named Tevye and his wife Golde live in a Russian village. Tevye tries to persuade his five daughters to follow the custom of his people and let a matchmaker choose their husbands. But none of his daughters want to go that route. He reluctantly gives approval to his second daughter to get married to a young man whom she says she loves. Then Tevye turns to Golde and asks her, "Do you love me?"

Golde responds to the question of whether she loves Tevye by telling him that for twenty-five years she has cooked his meals, cleaned the house, washed his clothes, slept with him, mothered their children, starved with him, lived with him, and fought with him. "If that's not love," she essentially declares, "then I don't know what it is." Then Tevye ask her again if she loves him. She responds, "I suppose I do." Then together they sing that after twenty-five years, expressions of love don't change anything. But they conclude that it is nice to know they love each other.[5]

What Is Love?

What is love? Love is the deepening of a relationship. Love is the act of bonding together where both husband and wife seek to help each other develop into all that is meant by authentic personhood. There is giving and receiving on the part of each partner. There is mutual sharing. The woman is not subordinate to the man; instead, each tries to bring fulfillment to the other. The union is both physical and spiritual and is not to be broken unless one partner dies.

Divorce Is a Reality

There is a note of pain in the words of Jesus. These words are evidence of a tear on God's cheek. They reflect a sob, a sigh within the heart of God. Why? Although Jesus states the ideal for marriage here, he knows that many fall far short of that ideal and that divorce does take place. It is a reality. We may not like it, but it happens. The divine intention in marriage, unfortunately, does not always occur. Because of "hardness of heart" or "stubbornness," God's will for marriage is often abated, and, like all sin, divorce rends the heart of God. It is against God's intention for man and woman to divorce.

Jesus' Teaching Is Not Legalism

Many make the mistake, I think, of trying to turn Jesus' teaching on divorce into another form of legalism. It is interesting how some people make Jesus more of a Pharisee than the Pharisees were. They try to make this teaching so absolutely binding that they do not believe a divorce should be granted for any reason other than adultery. These people take the words of Jesus in our passage literally. But they don't take Jesus literally when he said, "Give everything you have away to the poor and come follow me." They don't take him literally when he said, "When someone strikes you on one cheek, turn the other cheek." They don't take him literally when he said, "Cut off your hand if it offends you" or "Take up your cross and come follow me."

Are There Grounds for Divorce?

A number of years ago, a woman's husband murdered another man. Her husband pleaded insanity and was put in prison for life. Because of the English laws at that time, his wife could not divorce him. If the man had not been declared insane, he would have been executed and his wife would have been free to remarry. But at the time, this strange law forbade her to divorce him.

Are there ever grounds for divorce? What about a husband who habitually abuses his wife, physically or mentally? What does a spouse do with the discovery that his or her mate is homosexual? What does a spouse do if the marriage partner has a character or mental disorder or some other kind of problem? Are there never any grounds for divorce?

I think we need to understand that Jesus declared the indissolubility of marriage as the ideal from God's creation. But he was not trying to set up a more rigid legalism. Eduard Schweizer declares boldly that the whole section shows how unlegalistic Jesus is (Matt 19:10-12). He can speak with equal ease of the mystery of indissoluble marriage and of the mystery of celibacy.[6] Schweizer is affirming, in response to the disciples' question about whether it is better not to marry, it seems to me, that Jesus is stating that marriage or celibacy are ways one can serve God. Either marrying or remaining single is acceptable.

The Priority of Love

Look how Jesus responded to people when they were in trouble. He always upheld God's ideal. "Seek first the kingdom of God." "Be ye therefore perfect." But Jesus knows that no one ever seeks God's kingdom fully. He also knows none of us is perfect. We all fall short of the ideal. Notice how Jesus responded to the Samaritan woman at the well (John 4). He told her of the possibility that she could have "living water" gushing up within her that could give her eternal life. A woman who was caught in the act of adultery and was about to be stoned heard Jesus offer her forgiveness and say, "Go and sin no more" (John 8). Jesus ministered with the priority of love. He did not treat people as they deserved to be treated; he treated them according to unconditional grace.

We know that we all sin and fall short of God's ideal in many ways. When people fall short of this ideal, they sin. And then Jesus grants them forgiveness and grace. Jesus says that we are "to love God with all our heart, mind, soul, and strength. And we are to love our neighbor as ourselves" (Matt 22:36-40). The great commandment takes priority over other laws. Robert Sinks has expressed it this way: "Whenever marriage serves to crush what is genuinely human, then it must yield to the higher principle of the Great Commandment."[7] We are to love as God loves.

The Church's Position on Divorce and Remarriage

There are times when one person in a marriage is absolutely devastated by his or her partner. The ideal is not always realized, even for people who are Christians. Jesus was not one of the Pharisees; he fought their narrowness at every corner. What stance then should the church take regarding divorce and remarriage in the light of Jesus' teachings?

Teach the Ideal

First, I think the church needs to teach and preach clearly the ideal of marriage. We should proclaim that from creation God has desired that one man and one woman be bonded in a covenant with each another until death parts them. This is the Christian ideal. The church has fallen far short of teaching the Christian ideal of marriage. How many sermons have you heard about divorce? How many teachings and workshops do we have about Christian marriage today? We assume wrongly that our church people know what Christian marriage is. Simply because people get married in a church doesn't make their marriage Christian. We have failed in this area. We need to teach and preach more effectively what the Christian ideal is.

We need to remind people that Christ is Lord of our marriages as well as all of life.

Reach Out to the Divorced with Love

Second, when people fall in their marriages, rather than rejecting them, heaping guilt and scorn upon them, and increasing their pain, the church needs to reach out to them with love, care, acceptance, and grace. These people need someone to minister to them. I cannot tell you how many times people have told me they fear that they may be living in adultery because they have been divorced and have remarried, or they want to know if they will be committing adultery if they remarry.

What does the church often do? Sometimes the church heaps more guilt upon divorced people by quoting from this difficult saying of Jesus. Rather than crushing people with a load of guilt, the church needs to let them know that divorce is not the unpardonable sin. Like someone who has committed any other sin, a person who is divorced can experience forgiveness and grace from God and the opportunity to begin a new life.

Communicate that Divorce Is Not the Unpardonable Sin

James G. Emerson wrote some words that have been helpful to me:

> My argument is that not to recognize divorce is to deny the oneness of God's creation. It is to deny that what theology calls "the condition of sin" may have its effect in every area of life. To say that one hates divorce is not to say that divorce does not exist. A decision must still be made as to how to deal with that which does exist.[8]

This statement is further based on the argument that a marriage may die spiritually just as it may die physically. If remarriage can be granted upon physical death, then it must also be granted upon spiritual death.[9]

The church must hold up the Christian ideal of marriage and state that divorce is wrong. But divorce, like any other sin, can be forgiven. Divorced people, having experienced forgiveness, can now begin to rebuild their lives.

Offer Counseling and Divorce Support Groups

Third, the church needs to provide counseling and divorce support groups to help guide people during this difficult period. As a church family, we should say to people going through a divorce or already divorced that we still see them as people, as God's children, with special needs like all of us have that need to be met.

Bruce Fisher was divorced and noted fifteen issues that he and other people face in the trauma of divorce. The issues he addressed include denial, loneliness, rejection, guilt, grief, anger, letting go, problems with self-esteem, friendships, leftover feelings, love, trust, facing one's sexuality, responsibility when a person has been over-dependent or under-dependent, what to do with singleness and freedom.[10] Children of divorced families face many difficulties, including being deprived of one parent, parental quarreling, the disruption of moving, and many others.[11] The church needs to provide resources for divorced people and their families to help them deal with their struggles.

Proclaim the Inclusive Nature of God's Love

Fourth, the church needs to remind all people of the inclusive nature of God's love and the church's acceptance of everyone. No matter who you are, male or female, married or single, the church still reaches out its arms to you with a message of Christ's love and invites you to be a part of its fellowship. You are not rejected because you are single, divorced, or married. In Jesus Christ, there is neither male nor female, married nor single, slave nor free. We are one—brothers and sisters in Christ. Our goal is to grow toward full personhood to be like Christ.

Listen and Respond

Fifth, the church should listen more and respond to the needs, hurts, and pain of people who are divorced, in blended families, in the midst of a divorce, struggling as a single parent, or in any other circumstance related to divorce. Through our teaching and programs, we want divorced people and children of divorced parents to know we care and wish to help them. We should present the love and forgiveness of Christ and the opportunity to begin again with their lives. We must assure all people that the church is a place where they can express their hurt and anger, share their fears and tears, and still be accepted and loved.[12]

On one hand, the church must boldly and unapologetically lift up the ideal of marriage in which one man and one woman make a commitment to each other until death parts them. God ordained this indissoluble union in creation. This is the Christian ideal for marriage. We ought to teach it, guide people in understanding it, counsel them in living up to this standard, and direct them in its path.

On the other hand, facing the pain of the reality of how many people are divorced, we must reach out to divorced people to minister, care for, and love them, even as our Lord showed his love to all when he was on the earth. May we hear the words of Jesus that remind us that God *loved* the world. Looking to our Lord's example of love, may we try to be loving even as Christ has loved us.

Notes

1. "Six Surprising Facts about Divorce in 2017," Wevorce, wevorce.com/blog/6-surprising-divorce-statistics-divorce-2017/.

2. Richard P. Olson and Joe H. Leonard, Jr., *Ministry with Families in Flux* (Louisville: Westminster/John Knox Press, 1990) 9.

3. Sarah Jacoby, "Here's What the Divorce Rate Actually Means," *Refinery.com*, 2 February 2017, refinery29.com/2017/01/137440/divorce-rate-in-america-statistics.

4. William F. Luck, *Divorce and Remarriage* (San Francisco: Harper & Row, 1987) 107.

5. Stanley Richards, *The Best Plays of the Sixties* (Garden City NY: Doubleday, 1970) 308f.

6. Eduard Schweizer, *The Good News According to Matthew* (Atlanta: John Knox Press, 1977) 383.

7. Robert F. Sinks, "A Theology of Divorce," *Christian Century* (20 April 1977): 379.

8. James G. Emerson, Jr., *Divorce, the Church and Remarriage* (Philadelphia: The Westminster Press, 1961) 164.

9. Ibid.

10. Olson and Leonard, *Ministry with Families in Flux*, 43–44.

11. Ibid., 44.

12. For help in providing assistance to those in need, see David Instone Brewer, *Divorce and Remarriage in the Church: Biblical Solutions for Pastoral Relations* (Downers Grove: IVP Books, 2013); Rubel Shelly, *Divorce and Remarriage: A Redemptive Theology* (Abilene TX: Leafwood Publishers, 2007); Daniel G. Bagby, *Seeing Through Our Tears: Why We Cry, How We Heal* (Minneapolis: Augsburg, 1999); Wayne E. Oates, *Pastoral Counseling in Social Problems: Extremism, Race, Sex, Divorce* (Louisville: Westminster, 1986) 103–24.

10

When Jesus Doesn't Bring Peace

Matthew 10:34-39; 12:46-50

Jesus' words from Matthew 10:34, "You must not think that I have come to bring peace to the earth. I am not come to bring peace but a sword," are startling to those of us who remember reading this angelic message to the shepherds upon the birth of Christ: "Glory to God in the highest and peace on earth" (Luke 2:14). This text also seems in stark contrast to the words of Jesus when he said, "Blessed are the peacemakers" (Matt 5:9). I believe that these words of Jesus were intended to focus not on the purpose of his coming but on the effect that his coming might have within families and among friends. It is an abuse of this text, I think, to use it as a rallying cry for war. Some may say, "Jesus has called us to do battle, to meet the enemy with force." Armed with this thought, they go galloping off in some fanatical conquest.

If this is not Jesus' intention, then what does this strange text mean? The view that the Messiah came to bring strife was in conflict with the concept people in Jesus' day had of the Messiah. The standard view that people had of the Messiah was that he was to bring peace, not strife.

Religion Often Brings Conflict

Let's see if we can get a handle on the meaning of this Scripture. Notice first that it reminds us that religion often brings conflict. Jesus was telling his hearers clearly that his disciples would often find themselves in conflict with others, and sometimes they might be in conflict with those closest to them—the people in their own families. We sometimes sing, "Give me that old-time religion." You had better be careful if you want that old-time religion, because you might get it. You might get the religion of Abraham that caused him to leave his family and his country and go off to a strange place where he had never been as he followed God's leadership. His religion challenged him to go on a daring new venture. Do you really want that? "Give me that old-time religion of Moses," we sometimes sing. Do you really want the old-time religion of Moses? His religion caused him to stand up before the political forces of his day and cry, "Let my people go!" His faith in God put him in conflict with the political, military, and governmental forces of his day. Do you really want that kind of old-time religion? You may get the old-time religion of Jesus, which might put you in conflict with many today.

There is an interesting image of God in the book of Deuteronomy. God is depicted like an eagle (Deut 32:11). The eagle is sketched flying down and disturbing and eventually destroying the nest of its young so that the small eaglets will try to fly. If they fail in their first effort to fly, the eagle sweeps under them and catches them and supports them on its wings. The eagle stirs up the nest to force its young to grow and develop.

What is this image telling us? God doesn't always come into our lives to bring peace of mind or to make us feel good. God sometimes comes into our lives to stir us up. Do you think God can possibly be happy with the world the way it is? Our world is filled with wars, murders, rapes, robberies, and people in continuous conflict. Can God be pleased with this? I think God constantly comes into our lives and stirs us up to motivate us toward maturity. Religion often causes conflict in our personal lives, with the established government, with our own families, with other systems of authority around us, or with the values of our society. Through it all, we are challenged to be like God.

The Nature of the Christian Way

When Jesus called us to be his disciples and follow him, he didn't tell us about an easy or comfortable way in which we would live in air-conditioned buildings and sit on cushioned pews. Jesus did not hide the sharp "steel flint" in discipleship. Sometimes, he noted that his disciples would have to turn the other cheek or go the second mile or give somebody else their outer coat. Jesus spoke candidly about taking up one's cross to follow him and being faithful unto death. He made it clear that sometimes his way would be difficult. On some occasions his followers would be rejected rather than welcomed.

Look through the pages of Christian history and you will see again and again that Christians were indeed often rejected, misunderstood, abused, persecuted, and even martyred. When the early Christians gathered for worship, outsiders did not understand their observance of the Lord's Supper. Misunderstandings about "eating the body and drinking the blood of Jesus" in the Lord's Supper caused Christians to be accused of cannibalism. The celebration of their "Love Feast" led to accusations of immorality. Because the Christians had no images in their places of worship, they were accused of being atheists. Since they refused to bow down to the emperor or to an image of him, they were accused of not being patriotic. From Nero on, Christians have suffered through all kinds of persecution. Many Christians were put to death for their beliefs. Christians have indeed had to endure all kinds of abuse, misunderstanding, and persecution.

Being a Christian in One's Home

But in our text, Jesus states that sometimes the most difficult place to be a Christian may be within one's own home. Jesus, I think, may have been speaking autobiographically. Other passages of Scripture (Mark 3:21; Matt 12:46-50) state that Jesus' family came to one of the places where he was teaching because they wanted to take him home. They wanted to restrain him because they thought he was "beside himself" or insane. His own family did not understand him. They were not in agreement with his ministry. They thought that their older son, their elder brother, was demented. Sometimes our problems, like our Lord's, can be with our own families.

In the early church, this often became a real problem. A husband might become a Christian while his wife was a pagan. This set the family at odds with each other. What could they do? Great conflict often ensued. Paul writes some words regarding this situation in 1 Corinthians 7:12-16. Some scholars speculate that the Apostle Paul was likely married at one time because his position as a Pharisee usually required that one be married. Perhaps Paul's wife later abandoned or divorced him when he became a Christian. If Paul were married, as Pharisees usually were, and his wife deserted or divorced him after he became a Christian, this might explain why he stated that it was acceptable to marry one's fiancée, but he who refrains from marriage will do better (1 Cor 7:38). This, of course, is only speculation on my part. Other scholars have suggested that Paul's preference for celibacy and his encouragement that others might follow his example was strongly grounded in the view that the return of Christ would be in Paul's own lifetime.[1]

When one's family member became a Christian at the time of the early church, it often produced tremendous conflict. But this is not a conflict confined to the past. When I was in college, I was a summer missionary to Hawaii. A Buddhist young man became a Christian and was baptized and joined a local church. When he converted, his family rejected him forever! In some religious groups, when a person converts to another religion, that person is considered dead. The family literally has a funeral service for their family member, and he or she can no longer come home. The person is not considered a son or a daughter anymore and is excluded from the family. Sometimes the hardest place to be Christian, Jesus said, is within your own family.

"If you love your father or mother or any family member more than me, then you are not worthy of me," Jesus declared (Matt 10:37). Jesus Christ demands first place in your allegiance, first place above everyone—even your own family. In our American family tradition and in almost any tradition, that is difficult to accept. But Jesus states that his claim for loyalty overrides all others. "I am number one," he says. I know many ministers who labor their entire lives without any support from their own families. Their families do not understand or lend them any type of encouragement. Eugene Boring reminds us that "to be a disciple of Jesus is to belong to the wider family of the community of faith" and is not an individualistic matter.[2]

If we are going to follow Jesus, the answer is not peace at any price. Any Christian knows how difficult it is to try to talk to one's family members about Christ. Jesus has not called us to be his disciples at the cost of peace at any price. We have to learn to wage both war and peace. We have got to be willing to stand up for Christ, whether it is in business, at work, or even at home.

When William Wilberforce became a Christian, he began his efforts to stop the slave traffic in England. On one occasion, he was defeated in the British House of Commons. As he walked out the door of the House of Commons, he was met by a pious Christian who asked him, "Have you found peace, my brother?" "No, I am not at peace," Wilberforce said. "I've found war." There are times when the Christian doesn't need peace in his or her life. Instead, he or she needs to wage war against slavery, prejudice, and other forces of evil in the world. The Christian is not called to have peace at any price. This peace needs to be according to the will of Christ. Sometimes Jesus Christ brings conflict into our lives.

The Challenge of Choosing the Christ-like Way

Go with me a step further and see that Jesus is challenging his followers to make a choice. When Jesus Christ confronts us with his presence, we have to decide whether we are for him or against him. We have to decide whether we will follow him or reject him. Not to decide is to decide. Jesus says, "If you are not for me you are against me" (Matt 12:30). We can't be neutral; we must make a choice. We either follow Jesus or reject him. Jesus lifted himself up as the point of response. "I, if I be lifted up, I will draw all men unto me" (John 12:32). He is the central point of focus in directing us to God. Matthew uses an interesting image when he observes that Jesus' mother, brothers, and sister were "standing outside" the house where Jesus was teaching (Matt 12:46-50). Often there are people who stay outside and refuse to come into his presence and follow him. Jesus demands absolute allegiance. Down through the ages, individuals who have been willing to give Jesus absolute allegiance have seen their lives transformed and experienced redemption, purpose, and meaning.

E. Stanley Jones, the noted missionary and deeply devout Christian who shared the gospel of Christ with people around the world, once wrote, "I cannot go down any road with anybody who has problems without running into the necessity of self-surrender. All else is marginal, this is central. I have only one remedy, for I find only one disease—self at the center, self trying to be God."[3] Jesus calls us to surrender. The paradoxical fact is that we find victory through surrendering to Christ as Lord. When we crown him as Lord, we get out of our selfishness and we get into his way of life—the way of service.

When I was in Copenhagen several years ago, I had the opportunity to see several statues by noted Danish sculptor Thorwaldsen. One of Thorwaldsen's famous sculptures is an image of Christ at the center of the church with outstretched arms. As you walk close to this figure and get underneath the arms of Christ, you discover that you cannot see Jesus' face. A guide would instruct the visitors, "Kneel. Kneel at his feet. When you kneel, look up and you can see into his face." We see Jesus Christ not merely as an object for study or as someone to read about or sing about or hear preached about. We kneel in adoration at his feet. Then we rise up to follow Christ as Lord of our lives. We are challenged to make a choice.

The Paradox of the Cross

Go with me one more step and notice that Jesus sets forth the paradox of the cross: ". . . he who does not take up his cross and follow me is not worthy of me" (Matt 10:38-39). Jesus puts the primary focus on the cost of discipleship: one is not worthy of Christ if he or she refuses to take up the cross and follow him. The people in Jesus' day understood what that image meant. When a person was crucified, that individual often had to bear the crossbeam of his cross on his shoulder to the place where he was to die. He would literally struggle down the pathway with that heavy crossbeam on his shoulder. Sometimes he would fall; sometimes he was whipped as he walked along the way. When he reached the place of crucifixion, he was stretched out on that crossbeam and lifted up to die on the cross.

Jesus said to his disciples, "You must take up your cross." I do not think Jesus was referring here primarily to a wooden cross that one had to carry someplace. He was speaking about a way of life, a way of self-sacrifice, a way of spending one's life in service. Instead of seeking to save one's life, it is spent in ministry. Christ's way is giving instead of receiving, losing one's life in ministry for others instead of trying to hoard things for oneself. This is a call for sacrificing, giving, pouring out one's life in love. The call is not selfishly to see what one can get for oneself; it is to see what one can do for others. The challenge is to take up one's cross and go into the areas of life where there is human need and hurt.

For me, Albert Schweitzer has always been one of the paramount examples of self-sacrifice. Laying aside his noted career as a professor and musician, he studied and prepared to become a medical doctor. Then he went to Africa to serve in a "backwoods" spot of the world to help people in need. He ministered quietly to these people as a doctor and taught them about Christ. Someone asked him once why he made such a radical move. He said that he was stabbed awake one morning with the realization that

> I must not accept this happiness as a matter of course, but must give something in return for it. I tried to settle what meaning lay hidden for me in the saying of Jesus: "Whosoever would save his life shall lose it, and whosoever shall lose his life for my sake and the Gospels shall save it." . . . In addition to the outward, I now had inward happiness.[4]

He made a hard choice.

Not all of us have to go to Africa to fulfill this challenge. We can say that the Albert Schweitzers are rare. Yes, they are! But there are others who have walked the sacrificial way: Mother Teresa, Toyohiko Kagawa, Bill Wallace, Tom Dooley, Florence Nightingale, William Booth, Martin Luther King, Jr., and a host of others who have served God in a variety of sacrificial ways.

These are not the only individuals who have walked the paradoxical way of Christ. I can point to individuals I have known who served God sacrificially. Some have devoted their lives to Christ through churches where I have been pastor. They have served ten, fifteen, twenty, and some even fifty years as Sunday school teachers of boys and girls. Others have gone for years, ten years or more, to nursing homes in our city where they have led services of worship and have given love and care to people in need. I think of those who prepared meals and took them to shut-ins or to the homeless. I think of those who reached out to the hurting and needy in our community. Some worked in our Alzheimer's support group or with another special group in our church or community. These people have not focused on themselves and what life can do for them, but instead they have tried to focus on what they can do to serve God and help others. Many serve God quietly as they follow the way of the cross.

Leslie Weatherhead, the English preacher/pastor who was for many years at City Temple in London, has always been one of my favorite writers. In one of his last books, in the chapter titled "Christ and His Achievements," he penned these lines:

> It is with a sense of deep humility and reverence almost of awe, that I, having recently passed my seventieth birthday, sit down in this quiet study, within sight and sound of the sea, to write about the Person who has meant more to me than any other for over sixty years. As a child of nine, I made my little act of dedication to him all alone on January 3, 1903, and determined to serve him for the rest of my life. I remember writing down the fact in red ink in a new diary someone had given me. Needless to say, I have gone back on him a thousand times, but always he has held my heart in thrall and I have known no peace outside his will and no joy to compare with the experience which I sincerely believe to be due to communion with him.[5]

There is no greater joy and peace than in following Christ, sensing his impact on your life, and letting his standard guide you. Sometimes this discipleship means that it will be difficult to live with other people, even your own family, because they may misunderstand or reject you. Hopefully, out of love and concern you will continue to seek to draw them to Christ.

You do this not forcibly or in some artificial way, but gently and lovingly you reveal to them the way of Christ through your daily actions and words.

Two men had been business partners for twenty years. On Sunday morning, they always met on a commuter train. One of the partners was on his way to church, where he went every week. The other was going to play golf. After twenty years of meeting on the train like this, the man who was going to play golf said to his partner as he got ready to step off the commuter train, "Look here, when are you going to give up all this hypocrisy about religion and churchgoing?" "I don't understand you," his friend replied. "I mean just what I say: when are you going to give up this hypocrisy?" Deeply hurt, the partner answered, "What right have you to call my religion hypocrisy?" "Well," said the other, "we have been partners for twenty years. We have met and talked together every day. You know quite well that if what you profess to believe is true, it is a very hopeless case for me, and yet you have never said one word to help me to be anything different."

We wonder why individual churches don't grow more. The answer is simple. You and I haven't reached out to anybody! When was the last time you tried to invite someone to become a disciple of Jesus? When was the last time you took up your cross and went someplace for Christ? The preacher can't do it for you. The staff of a local church can't do it. All of us are charged to take up our cross and reach others for Christ. Some of us never even invite people to our church. Jesus calls us to love him more than any other. He demands first allegiance. And if he has that allegiance from us, then surely we will want to share that joy with others.

Notes

1. For further discussion see Manfred T. Branch, *Hard Sayings of Paul* (Downers Grove: Intervarsity Press, 1989) 108ff; A. N. Wilson, *Paul: The Mind of the Apostle* (New York: W. W. Norton & Co., 1997) 138ff; Holmes Rolston, *The Social Message of the Apostle Paul* (Richmond VA: John Knox Press, 1942) 107ff.

2. M. Eugene Boring, "The Gospel of Matthew," *The New Interpreter's Bible* (Nashville: Abingdon Press, 1995) 298.

3. E. Stanley Jones, *Victory through Surrender* (Nashville: Abingdon Press, 1966) 14.

4. Albert Schweitzer, *Out of My Life and Thought* (New York: Holt, Rinehart and Winston, Inc., 1961) 85.

5. Leslie Weatherhead, *The Christian Agnostic* (New York: Abingdon Press, 1965) 93.

11

The Hand that Offends You

Matthew 5:29-30

The novelist Petru Dumitriu tells an interesting story about a man named Panait Petre who was a forester. Panait worked in the deep woods and felled giant trees for profit. Long wooden shoots had been constructed in the mountain forest for sliding the tree logs down the slopes into the waters below. The wooden shoots were polished smooth inside so the logs would slide down quickly. Foresters would sometimes slide down the polished surface themselves rather than walk. One day Panait was using the slide like a toboggan to get to the bottom of the hill. His foot went through a knothole in the slide and he was caught. Someone yelled a warning that a tree trunk was coming down the shoot toward him. He knew his life was threatened. He struggled but could not free his foot. In an instant, he made a decision. He took his ax and cut off his foot to save his life.

In the fifth chapter of Matthew's Gospel we read these difficult words from Jesus: "If your right eye is your undoing, tear it out and fling it away; it is better for you to lose one part of your body than for the whole of it to be thrown into hell. And if your right hand is your undoing, cut it off and fling it away; it is better for you to lose one part of your body than for the whole of it to go into hell" (Matt 5:29-30). Mark also adds "foot" in his Gospel. This is not an easy text either to read or understand.

In the day when Jesus lived, many people believed that the strongest sinful impulses resided in the hand, eye, or foot. Sometimes, rather than being executed, criminals had one of their body parts removed or amputated for a crime. For example, a thief who had stolen something might lose a hand as punishment. He then went through life with his hand missing as a sign to everybody that he was a thief. Within Judaism, however, there were strong religious convictions against any kind of self-mutilation. So Jesus' words would have sounded strange coming from a religious leader.

I do not believe we are to take this text literally. Even those who want to force Bible literalism on others do not seem to take this passage literally. I haven't seen many one-eyed and one-armed men and women in church. Have you? That's because we don't take this text literally. But I know that many people have seen things with their eyes or done things with their hands or feet that have been offensive. Actually, most of us have. But we have not taken Jesus' words literally and gouged out our eyes or cut off our hands.

What are we to do with this text?

It's a Radical Demand to Follow Jesus

Let's try to capture the real meaning of Jesus' words. Jesus is telling us clearly in this text, as he does in many others, that to follow him is a radical demand. "You must be willing to make any sacrifice to follow me," Jesus says. This demand is absolute and unconditional. "If your right eye is your undoing or proves to be a stumbling block, tear it out and throw it away," he urges. The word in Greek for "stumbling block" is the root for our English word "scandal." This word for stumbling block could be a reference to a large stone in a person's path that might cause him or her to stumble. Or the word was sometimes used to refer to a trap set across a path or to a deep pit that had been dug and covered over in order to fool and trap a traveler. The point is that this "stumbling block" is something that trips a person and causes him or her to come to a destructive end. Jesus states that if your eye is your undoing, then you need to throw it away. It is better to lose part of one's body than keep one's whole body and be cast into Gehenna.

Gehenna was literally a place located south and west of Jerusalem. It was the city's garbage dump. The garbage of the city was cast into Gehenna and left burning all the time. It was a place where worms and insects bred to decompose the castaways and where wild dogs fed. Gehenna became the symbol of eternal hell in Judaism. Jesus warns his hearers, "Make a radical decision. You don't want to be cast on the garbage dump, so choose life." We each make a choice. We can choose the way of Christ that leads to life or we can choose the way that leads to the garbage dump and destruction. We must make a choice, and not choosing is making a choice!

Instruments in Our Sinfulness

Jesus says that our eye might offend us. David's eye was his undoing. The Scriptures state that David came out onto his roof porch one day and saw Bathsheba bathing at her house. He continued to look at her until he lusted after her. Sometimes we engage our hands in certain activities that lead us into the paths of sin, or our feet carry us down pathways that lead us away from God. Our eyes, hands, or feet become instruments in our own destruction.

Jesus knew far better than you or me that the seat of our sinfulness resides deep within, in our minds or hearts. Our eye, hands, feet, or any other part of our body sins because the original motivation for sin comes from within. Jesus states this clearly in many other places. But the eye, the hand, or the feet are instruments in carrying out our sinfulness. Jesus states that sometimes radical surgery is necessary to cut out our sinful behavior. In order to save his or her life, a person might have to sacrifice a member of the body. This part of our body is precious to us and it will be painful to give it up. To lose a limb of the body is not an easy sacrifice. But this figurative sacrifice is sometimes necessary in order to save a person's life.

Remove Anything that Hinders Following Jesus

If we are to find life, there are certain things we need to cut away, root out, or subtract. I can't tell you exactly what these may be in your life. But surely there are some things that every one of us needs to cast away from our lives or cut out of our lives. Whatever hinders you from fully following Christ needs to be removed or cut away. This may be painful or difficult, but it is necessary if your life is to be saved. For some, what needs to be removed is the control of drugs that have taken over them. For others, it is the abuse of alcohol. For others, it is an excessive appetite for material things or for pleasure. For others, it is jealousy, revenge, greed, envy, bitterness, prejudice, malice, hatred, bad temper, constant criticism, negative attitudes, the inability to see anything good in anyone else. If one or more of these are dominating your relationships to others, they need to be cut out of your life. Anything that hinders your relationship to God and anything that hinders you from growing and developing in healthy ways toward others needs to be cut out of your life. Anything that keeps us from following our Lord's leadership needs to be removed.

The Good May Keep Us from Reaching for the Best

Sometimes even the good needs to be cut out so we can acquire the best. Our jobs, which may be good, may also demand so much time that we never have any left to give to our families. We need to prioritize our time. Some people give so much attention to reaching material ends and making themselves comfortable that they do nothing to develop the spiritual sides of their lives and are empty and void within. If teachers begin to call attention to themselves rather than the subjects they teach, they have lost sight of their priorities. Whenever a preacher or any minister begins to get in the way of other people worshiping God, then something is wrong with that minister. A minister ought to be transparent so that people can come directly to God. It is wrong to spend time calling attention to ourselves. Even if our talents are good and worthy of praise, if they hinder instead of enhance someone's relationship to God, they need to be cut off.

Following Christ is costly, as we read in many places in Matthew. Jesus uses the image of a man selling everything in order to purchase a pearl of great price (Matt 13:45). He cautions that we cannot serve two masters (6:24). He says in another place, "If you don't love father and mother more than me, you are not worthy of me" (10:37). He challenges us, "Seek first the kingdom of God" (6:33). Jesus' claim is radical. It is absolute and unconditional. Jesus must be first. How can we fulfill such a challenge? Let me suggest briefly three ways.

Have the Courage to Follow Christ

First, doing what Jesus talks about in our text requires courage. It took unbelievable courage for the lumberjack I mentioned earlier to cut off his foot. I don't know if I could have done that! But he saved his life. It takes unbelievable courage to stand up for Christian convictions—in the office, on the playground, or at home. When we stand up for Christ, we may be misunderstood, criticized, ridiculed, or ostracized. This doesn't mean we go around wearing a badge reading, "I'm a Christian. Are you?" It simply means we seek to live a Christ-like life every day. But that's not always easy. You know it and I know it.

A young teenager said he learned how to respond to those who were trying to push drugs on him at school. He would say, "I don't have any money today," and they would stop bothering him. Seeing this young man's example, others begin choosing to walk away when asked to buy drugs. It is easy to get pulled into what everybody else is doing and follow the crowd. Much of television and movies are loaded with messages of sexual license.

"Do whatever makes you feel good," they seem to say. It is hard for young people to withstand that kind of pressure. But many do. I know a man who had strong convictions about not serving alcohol. When he was told that he had to serve alcohol in his restaurant, he resigned and gave up his job. He was out of work for a long time, but he stood up for what he believed.

Christian courage is not always easy. Christian courage is not whistling in the dark. It is confronting problems. Christian courage is not sticking your head in the sand and ignoring difficulties. It is standing up and facing them. Christian courage is not assuming that everything is always okay no matter what. It is dealing with the harsh realities of everyday living. Christian courage is not wishing away your fears. It is meeting them with hope for the future. Christian courage is the willingness to stand for what is right, knowing that it is easier to yield to temptations. Christian courage is not a vain hope but the assurance that God stands beside us to strengthen us no matter what. "I can do all things through Christ who strengthens me," Paul said (Phil 4:13).

Have the Discipline to Follow Christ

Following Christ takes courage, but it also takes discipline. If there is an unpopular word today, it is "discipline." We are living in a time, more so than I have ever noticed before, when people do not want anything to do with discipline. People today want to be informal and laid-back. They don't want restrictions or restraints. They don't want anybody telling them what they should do. "I want to do whatever I want to do, anytime I want to do it, anyplace I want to do it," these people say. "I want to be free. I want to be me." This is the generation that wants to be free of any restraints. But friends, none of us will be completely free of restraints. Either we learn to discipline ourselves or society will discipline us. We do not have total freedom to do anything we want, anyplace, anytime. It is untrue to think anyone does.

Nothing worthwhile in life comes without some kind of discipline. If you are going to be educated, it requires discipline. You have to study. If you are going to learn a language in school, it takes discipline to acquire it. If you are going to have any kind of career, it takes discipline. Whether you are going to learn to be a stenographer, handle a new computer, or operate heavy road equipment, it takes discipline and time. If you are going to be an attorney, a doctor, a dentist, a musician, or an athlete, it takes discipline. No one reaches a high goal simply by saying, "I want to do that thing."

In one church where I was the pastor, one of our high school students broke the record in Virginia for long-distance running. He didn't accomplish that by getting up one morning and saying, "You know, I am going to run today and break the state record." How did he do it? He got up every day and started running a short way, then went a little farther the next day and the next, until finally he reached the point where he was able to run fifteen miles every day. Then he ran those fifteen miles day after day, week after week. He disciplined his body and his time to reach his desired goal.

We want to do many things in life, but we are often unwilling to discipline ourselves to achieve them. It takes discipline to reach any worthwhile goal. A marriage vow requires discipline. Each marriage partner promises to the other to pledge his or her life, honor, love, and faithfulness. Love requires discipline. Love requires us to narrow our focus on an individual we are reaching out to with compassion and grace. Discipline enables us to follow Christ because we seek to understand what Christ's way is, what his view of life is, and how to incorporate his lifestyle into our lives. This can only come through prayer, Bible study, and worship as we seek to model our lives after Christ. We can't do this without discipline. Christ's way is demanding, narrow, and focused.

Have the Faith to Follow Christ

Third, the radical discipleship of Christ requires faith. This step begins with faith in oneself. A lot of people do not have much faith in themselves. I like the words from Tennyson about the person who was "loyal to the royal" in himself (in his poem *To the Queen*). Shakespeare puts these words on the lips of Polonius in *Hamlet*: "To thine own self be true, / And it must follow, as the night the day, / Thou canst not then be false to any man." Learn to be true to the authentic self within you. Remember that you have been created in the image of God, which means you were made a little less than God. You are modeled after God, and you need to be true to your high self that reflects the image of the God who made you. Let your conscience be modeled after Christ, who can strengthen you within to withstand those who criticize or challenge your convictions.

On a college campus several years ago, a lot of students got in trouble because of a cheating scandal. The president called an honor student into his office and asked him why he let himself get involved in this campus ruckus. "Sir," the student replied, "I'll bet you can't name ten men on this campus who would not have done exactly what I did under the circumstances." "Young man," the president responded, "has it occurred to you that you might have been one of those ten?" Why can't we stand up for the highest and best within us instead of giving way to what everybody else is doing?

Begin by having faith in yourself, and then have faith in others. I am convinced that some people do not have much faith in other people. In one of my favorite theological works, *Peanuts*, Lucy and Linus are talking one day, and Linus asks her, "Why are you always so anxious to criticize me?" "I just seem to have a knack for seeing other people's faults," Lucy replies. Then Linus asks, "What about your own faults?" "Oh," she says, "I have a knack for overlooking them."

Isn't that true of all of us? It is easy to see the faults in others, but we have a hard time seeing the faults in ourselves. When you read the New Testament, notice how Jesus responded to sinners. Rather than focusing on their sin or weaknesses, Jesus could see the potential good within them. Jesus would forgive them of their sins and encourage them. Look at that group of disciples: Simon Peter, Matthew, John, and the others. Who were these people? They seemed like nobodies. And yet these men and women who followed Christ were the ones to change the course of the world. Even in the midst of their difficulties and shortcomings, Jesus saw what they could become. Richard Foster, a Quaker and writer, challenged self-help guru Thomas Harris's concept, "I'm OK—you're OK." Foster turned it around and said, "You're not OK and I'm not OK but that's OK." He acknowledged that we are all sinners. There are faults and weaknesses within all of us, but in God's grace we can find wholeness and completeness. Christ was able to see the potential within us.

I am glad somebody could see possibilities in me. At one time in my life, it was probably difficult to see them. When I was in high school, I wasn't very interested in studying. I would sit in some of my classes and read other books. I always loved to read, but I didn't care what the teacher was talking about in the subject I was supposed to be studying. So I didn't do well in some of those courses. After I became a Christian and felt a call into ministry, I knew I needed to go to college. I had an abysmal high school record because up to that point I hadn't cared! Fortunately, there was a small junior college in Virginia where the admission folks said, "We'll give you a chance. You can enter on probation. You have to do well or you can't stay." That small junior college—Bluefield College—gave this guy, who had not done well in high school, an opportunity to go to college. They had faith in me. The dean later said that I was the only student who had come in on probation and later graduated in the honor society. I wasn't going to let them down. They had faith in me. We all need to experience the faith that others have in us, and we need to have faith in others too.

Finally, we need faith in God. We can never have enough strength within our own resources to meet all of life's challenges and difficulties. We have to lean on God for supportive strength. A small boy fell out of his bed one night, and his father went rushing into the room and asked, "Son, what happened?" "I don't know, Dad," the boy responded. "I guess I just fell asleep too close to where I got in!"

Many of us live our lives of faith too close to where we got in. We haven't matured and grown in our faith. We have remained close to the edge where we began our pilgrimage. If we are going to be able to follow Jesus Christ and meet the radical demands of discipleship, it is necessary for us to mature spiritually. As we grow deeper in our spiritual lives, faith will become a footbridge over the chasm of doubts and uncertainties we face. Faith will provide a path through the steep mountain range of all kinds of difficulties through which we must pass. Faith will be a light through a dark night of suffering and pain. Faith will be an anchor in the violent storms of our searching for and pursuing meaning in life. Faith will also be a shield against the fierce winds of temptations that confront us. Faith will be a quiet harbor after a perilous journey through a sea of personal problems and perplexities. At the same time, faith will be a tender hand to guide us into the way everlasting. We will also discover that faith is like a leap of absolute trust into the ocean of the unknown universe that lies before us. Faith is complete trust in God. Faith is relying on the strength of God when we become aware that our own strength is not enough.

I love the story about a small boy who was sent by his father to get logs for the fireplace. As the boy came into the den, he looked like he was going to drop the logs on the floor. His father asked him, "Son, why didn't you use all of your strength?" The small boy was hurt by that question from his father. But before he could respond, his father reached down and picked up his son along with the logs in his arms and said, "Son, you didn't ask me for help."

All of our strength is not within ourselves. We need to reach out in faith to experience the strength we can have from God. If we genuinely want to follow Jesus' radical call to discipleship as set forth in our text, we will hear our Lord's call that the life he offers is worth any sacrifice. If we want to make that kind of sacrifice, it will require courage, discipline, and faith. Are we really willing to make that kind of commitment? I pray that we are.

12

Is It Possible to Live by the Golden Rule?

Matthew 7:12

"I really don't believe in this religious stuff," the man said. "It's enough just to practice the Golden Rule." His friend quickly observed, "Yes, I agree with that, too. And I have my version of the Golden Rule, which is, 'Do unto others before they do unto you.'"

We encounter that kind of attitude all too often. Unfortunately, too many people have their own version of the Golden Rule. These people want their religion in small capsules. They prefer it simply to be a slogan. They would like to be able to write that slogan on a 3x5 card that they can stick in their pocket. They want religion to be summarized in one biblical verse or briefly stated in three easy points or in some sweet expression they can tape on the refrigerator. They want a simple faith that can be reduced to the barest essentials and stated or categorized easily. Some view the Golden Rule as the surest way to grasp everything a person needs to know about religion.

Many New Testament scholars have described Jesus' words known as the Golden Rule—"Treat others as you would have them treat you"—as the epitome of his teachings. Others have seen this rule as the key or summary of his teachings, while others called it the capstone or Mt. Everest of Jesus' ethical thought. In some sense, all of this may be true.

Not Original with Jesus

But in case you are not aware of it, you need to understand that this statement known as the Golden Rule was not original with Jesus. It has been found in other rabbinical teachings. It is seen in the writings of other rabbis, though mostly in a negative form. A famous rabbi named Shammai was noted for his stern and rigid disposition. One time a heathen came to Shammai and told him that if he could teach him all the essence of the law while he was standing on one foot, he would be received as a proselyte. Shammai ran the man off with a stick. Then the heathen went to Hillel, another noted rabbi. He repeated the same challenge to him. Hillel's response was, "What is hateful to yourself, do to no other. That is the whole law, and the rest is commentary." In the *Book of Tobit*, Tobias teaches his son what is really necessary to experience in life: "What thou thyself hatest, to no man do." There is another Jewish work called "The Letter to Aristeas" that is supposed to be an account about a Jewish scholar who went to Alexandria to translate the Hebrew Scriptures into Greek. At a banquet, the Egyptian king asked him a difficult question: "What is the teaching of wisdom?" "As you wish that no evil should befall you, but to be a partaker of all good things," the scholar replied, "so you should act on the same principle towards your subjects and offenders, and you should mildly admonish the noble and the good."

The Golden Rule has been noted in the works of other religious and philosophical teachers. In the writing of Confucius, the religious thinker is asked if there is one word that might guide a person in the rule of practice for his or her life. Confucius says, "Is not reciprocity such a word? What you do not want done to yourself, do not do to others." Epictetus also condemns slavery on the same principle. "What you avoid suffering yourselves, seek not to inflict upon others." The ancient Stoics had a proverb: "What you do not wish to be done to you, do not do to anyone else." A Hindu teacher taught, "Men gifted with intelligence and purified souls should always treat others as they themselves wish to be treated." From India, a Jainist wrote, "A man should wander about treating all creatures in the world as he himself would be treated." In the teachings of the Taoists there is the following statement: "Regard your neighbor's gain as your own gain, and regard your neighbor's loss as your own loss." There is a sense of universality about this teaching that has permeated many religions and philosophies through the ages.

A Positive Religion

There is then no need to claim that this is an absolutely new teaching from Jesus. Many religious leaders have put the Golden Rule in a negative form, but others, Jesus among them, express it in a positive way. Many of the scribes and Pharisees thought that religion was primarily a focus on refraining from certain things. If you do not murder, if you do not steal, if you do not commit adultery, then you are religious. Religion is determined by what you do *not* do. There are a lot of people today, including some church people, who see religion primarily as what they don't do. They assume that if a person doesn't do this thing or the other thing, he or she is religious. But are they really?

I love the story about a man who was talking one day with a neighbor who was trying to persuade him to join his congregation. "If I come to your church," the man asked, "what will I have to do?" "Well," his neighbor replied, "here is the list of the things you must not do to be a member of this church." The man listened for a while to his neighbor, grinned, and then said, "Oh, that is interesting." He had been walking his dog while he was listening to his neighbor. He pointed down to his dog and said, "See Spot sitting there waiting patiently while we talk? Spot doesn't do any of the things on your list either. But I don't think he is religious! I don't want to go to a church that primarily focuses on the things you should not do."

Jesus put this truth in a positive way. He taught us what we *should* do. To try to get a handle on this teaching from Jesus, let's begin with a negative note. Unfortunately, the Golden Rule has been used in a way that reveals deficiencies and abuses. To begin with, let's acknowledge that this saying from Jesus, "Do unto others as you would have them do unto you," does not contain the full essence of one's relationship to God. The Golden Rule is not a summary of the whole teachings of Jesus. It may be a key into our relationship with others. It may indeed be a summary of how we are to relate to others, but this teaching says nothing about our personal relationship to God. It does not address worship, prayer, or spiritual growth. It says nothing about the cross, the many other teachings of Jesus, his death, his resurrection, the Holy Spirit, or the church. It is not the whole truth about God. It is only a partial rule to guide us in our daily living. Some want to make this partial truth the whole truth. They claim that if you follow this teaching, you have fulfilled the requirements of the faith. But have you? You and I know better, don't we?

A Disguise for Selfish Behavior

Some people use the Golden Rule as a kind of disguise for selfish, inferior, or even evil behavior. They turn it around to say something like this: "I don't want anybody telling me what to do, and I'm not going to tell anybody else what to do." "I think taking drugs is fine because I get stimulated and motivated by them. So it is okay for others to use them too." "I get my highs from alcohol, so it is okay for others to drink to excess, too." "I ask nothing from others, and I give nothing in return." "I like to be flattered. It makes me feel worthwhile, so why not flatter other people?" "I don't forgive other people, so why should I want anybody to forgive me?"

Sometimes we base our attitude toward others on a bad premise, and we try to twist the Golden Rule into whatever we want to make it. Some have done this. They have let their consciences be their guide. And heaven forbid what some people's consciences tell them to do!

Not a Motive for Reward

Some people use the Golden Rule as a sort of a reward technique. They declare, "I will do good for you. By doing something good for you, I expect that you will in turn do something good for me." "I'll be nice to you, so you will be nice to me." Their action looks for something in return. They seek to gain something. They assume that "it pays to serve Jesus." This kind of attitude is expressed in a negative way toward God when a person gets ill or suffers and asks, "What have I done to deserve this?" "Who have I wronged?" "What did I ever do to other people that God is doing this to me?" Such people have lived their Christian lives in expectation of being rewarded in some way by God. Their desire to serve others is not from an unselfish motivation but from a longing for some kind of reward they think they deserve.

Not Just a Lesson about Morality

Some people say this teaching is primarily a lesson about morality. They think it focuses only on how we treat other people, that it is an ethical precept that has nothing to do with religion. To these folks, the basic point in life is that we get along with other people. If we can live in harmony, that is all we need to know about life.

A Guide for Living

Obviously, there are ways to twist or distort Jesus' teaching and turn it in almost any direction we want it to go. But how can we understand and live by what Jesus actually meant when he said, "Do unto other people as you would have them do unto you"? Might we begin by acknowledging that Jesus is providing a guide for relating to other people? First, the Golden Rule is a challenge to put ourselves in somebody else's place. Before we respond to another person, let's try to put ourselves in that individual's place. That is certainly not easy to do. Jesus is telling us that what we need is not more scholarly knowledge. We all know how we would like to be treated. The challenge is to look at somebody else before we act and ask ourselves, "Would I want this done to me if I were in that person's place?"

We need to acknowledge at the outset that it is not easy to get inside somebody else's mind or skin. To do this, imagine that you are a black man or woman who lived in the fifties in the American South. Consider the reaction black people often encounter today when they are pulled over by the police or mistreated in restaurants or other public establishments. If you are white, what would it be like to wake up in a world where your race no longer conferred privilege? You might have to live someplace else; you might not have the same job. A lot of factors in your life would be different. If you are white and are in conversation with a person of color, listen closely. Try to put yourself in that person's place. We have to confess that it is not easy to get into the mind of somebody else. We seldom can truly grasp their feelings. But we must try.

As another example, suppose you saw your neighbor's house being robbed. What would you do? You could have several responses. One attitude might be, "Well, it's not my house. Too bad for them! I'm not going to get involved in this. If they know I called the police, then they might do something to me." If, however, you really put yourself in the place of your neighbor, you would ask yourself, "What would I want somebody to do for me?" You know what your answer would be. You would dial 911 quickly! You would inform the operator that someone is breaking into your neighbor's house. By putting yourself in your neighbor's place, you know what you would want to be done for you. You value his or her rights as your own.

Called to a Higher Way

Jesus never said this way was easy. He lifted up this teaching like a blazing torch that throws light on a higher plain where we can walk. Jesus challenges us to move from a lower trail, marked by self-interest, to a higher realm marked by focus on others.

Several years ago, an airplane crashed into the Potomac River near Washington, DC. Helicopters were used to rescue several people from the cold water. One of the helicopters lowered a rope twice to a flight attendant trapped in the water. She tried to grasp the rope, but she was so weak that she slipped and fell back into the water each time. It looked like she would drown. A twenty-eight-year-old man named Lenny Skutnick was standing on the riverbank watching. After witnessing what was happening, he took off his coat, kicked off his boots, and jumped into the freezing water. He swam thirty yards to where the flight attendant struggled and tied the rope around her so she could be pulled up into the helicopter. Later, when the press asked him why he did what he did, he said, "I had been there all that time and nobody was getting in the water. . . . It's something I never thought I would do, but in looking back, I guess I did it because I didn't think about it. Somebody had to go in the water."

What was going on in this man's mind? Without saying it, he was likely thinking, "If I were there in the water and couldn't make it, I would want somebody to come and help me." He saw a need and went to help. Jesus said we are to try to put ourselves in somebody else's place. It is not always easy to do this, but it is our challenge.

The Teaching Is Linked to the Teacher

If we are going to practice the Golden Rule, we must recognize that this teaching has to be related to the Teacher. The resources for living this teaching are realized in one's allegiance to the Teacher. The reason some people distort this teaching or cannot live it out is they have rejected the Teacher. The Golden Rule is impossible to practice without the guidance of the Teacher. When Jesus was asked what was the greatest of all the commandments, he said, "You shall love the Lord your God with all your heart, mind, soul, and strength." Then he added, "The second is like it. You will love your neighbor as yourself." We can't really love our neighbor properly without being vitally related to God. Our relationship to God gives us the strength, power, guidance, and motivation to reach out and love others. We cannot begin with our neighbor. We begin with God. We cannot really love our neighbor until we love God.

This teaching begins with a connection, "Therefore . . . ." This word connects the lesson with what has come before it.

The Golden Rule is connected with Jesus' words about the way we pass judgment on other people. In the midst of this discussion about judgment Jesus says, "Ask and you will receive. Seek and you will find. Knock and the door will be opened. For everyone who asks, receives. The one who seeks, finds, and to the one who knocks, the door will be opened." What has prayer got to do with the teaching on the Golden Rule? Everything! We can't possibly treat others as we want them to treat us unless we are relating to the eternal God who strengthens us to implement this teaching. We have to ask God for strength and guidance. We must knock at the door of prayer for directions. We must keep seeking to have the necessary strength and fortification to live out this teaching.

A noted rabbi named R. Jochannan ben Zakkai sent five of his young pupils to inquire from some other rabbis what they thought was the true way to live if one was to attain the highest level in life. One rabbi told them they need "a good eye"; another said "a good friend"; another said "a good neighbor." One of them said, "He that foresees what it is to be." Ele'azar ben 'Arak said, "a good heart." Zakkai said to his pupils, "I approve the words of 'Arak rather than your words because his words include your words."[1]

If you and I have a heart that is related correctly to God, then everything else will fall into place. Our relationship to God will direct us in serving God effectively.

A Practical Teaching

To live out the Golden Rule, we have to realize that this teaching is meant to be practical. The Golden Rule was not meant to be admired or praised. It is not enough to exclaim, "Isn't this a wonderful principle?" It is a teaching that we are supposed to incorporate into our lives. We are supposed to live it, not just discuss it, debate it, or teach it. We are to practice it in our lives daily. That is where it gets difficult. The focus is not on what to know but what to do.

In one *Peanuts* comic strip, Charlie Brown and Linus are watching Snoopy sitting in the snow shivering on a cold, snowy day. Charlie Brown observes, "Snoopy looks kind of cold, doesn't he?" "I'll say he does," Linus observes. "Maybe we'd better go over and comfort him." So they walk over to Snoopy, leaning down to him where he is shivering in the snow and cold. "Be of good cheer, Snoopy," Linus says. "Yes," Charlie Brown says. "Be of good cheer." In the last frame, they are seen walking away and Snoopy is left sitting and shivering in the snow with a big question mark over his head.

The message in this comic is clear. Our religion is not just words. Genuine religion leads to action. We are called to live out this teaching in our daily lives. Jesus challenges his disciples to reach out to people who have needs to show love and concern to them. He lifts up the Good Samaritan as an example of authentic religion because the Samaritan demonstrated genuine religion by showing mercy to someone in need. His religion took on life. Too many people want to discuss religion, debate religion, think about religion, and pray about religion, but they don't want to live out their faith.

Jesus has reminded us that our service to others is rendered unto him. "When you have done it unto the least of these, you do it unto me." Matthew 25 quotes Jesus as affirming that when someone visits a person in prison, gives a cup of cold water, clothes the naked, or feeds the hungry, they are ministering to him. People might ask, "Lord, when did we minister to you?" Jesus says, "When you have done it unto the least of these, you have done it even also unto me." Ministering to people in their times of need is ministering to Christ.

Not an Easy Way

I suppose among the many frustrations in trying to be the church is our discovery that most people are unconcerned about the poor, the destitute, the unemployed, the homeless, the needy, or those who are victims of war. We want to know how we can get more material possessions. How can I get a new computer, a smart phone, a second car, a new house? How can I have more money in the bank? We want more of this and more of that. We are more concerned about the accumulation of things and less concerned about people. Dostoevsky, in his book *Brothers Karamazov*, has a powerful line: "Love in action is a too harsh and dreadful thing, compared with love in dreams."[2] It is easy to talk about Christian love in the abstract, but it is difficult to live out this love in our lives in the ways we respond to other people every day, especially when some people are difficult, obnoxious, evil, or hateful.

Donald H. Tippett, a former Methodist bishop, had one eye that was badly drooped. Ernest Campbell asked a friend how Tippett's eye was injured. The story and what follows are quite remarkable. Years ago, Tippett was a pastor in New York City. Two young men planned a robbery in upstate New York, and, in order to establish an alibi, they came by to visit the minister. While they were chatting with him, the pastor had to take a telephone call in another room. The young men were fearful that he was suspicious of them, and they jumped him in his office and beat him so badly with brass knuckles that they mangled his left eye. Later, when they were captured, Tippett pleaded for the young men and got their sentences reduced. He visited them in prison and helped them plan their future. He helped support one of them through college and then through medical school. That young man later became an ophthalmologist. Although Tippett did not find the Christian way always easy or even safe, he demonstrated through his life the power of Christian love along the narrow way of Christ.

If you asked Tippett if the religious way was easy or always safe, he would tell you no. Sometimes the way is harsh and difficult. The Golden Rule is a practical way of living out the words of Jesus: "A new commandment I give unto you, that you love one another as I have loved you" (John 13:34). This will sometimes entail courage on our part to try to get inside the head and skin of another person and understand them and their needs. The way of the Golden Rule is not easy. But through this teaching, Jesus was trying to enable us to know how to love our neighbors as ourselves. This maxim rests on our desire to love God with all of our heart, soul, mind, and spirit. No, following the Gold Rule is not easy. I suppose that is the reason we seldom see it lived out in life.

Notes

1. T. W. Manson, *The Teachings of Jesus* (Cambridge: Cambridge University Press, 1963) 307.

2. Fyodor Dostoevsky, *Brothers Karamazov* (Garden City NY: International Collectors Library, n.d.) 50.

13

Who Can Be Perfect?

Matthew 5:47-48

The statement from Jesus that we are to "be perfect as our Father in heaven is perfect" is troubling for all of us. After all, this command makes our spiritual growth seem like a hopeless undertaking. We know that none of us is ever perfect. If it's hopeless, why try at all? It is an impossible demand. This requirement makes me feel like a small child who has just learned the multiplication tables and someone says to me, "Now do some quantum physics." We can't begin to know where to begin. How can we possibly be perfect like God?

A Lesson from Jonathan Livingston Seagull

When I read Matthew 5:47-48 recently, it brought to my mind a small book that I had read several years ago titled *Jonathan Livingston Seagull* by Richard Bach. This short book received all kinds of interesting responses when it was first published. A bishop said that it was sheer heresy because it was nothing but a focus on pride. The director of the FBI wanted all of his agents to read it because he thought it would provoke motivation and enthusiasm within them. Some manufacturers wanted their salesmen to read it because it would inspire them to be better salesmen. The *Christian Science Monitor* refused even to take advertisements for the book. *Time* magazine did a major article on it, and so did *Theology Today*. This small book became a national best seller and has sold millions of copies. Though I haven't looked recently, I would suspect it is still in print, whether it deserves to be or not.

Jonathan Livingston Seagull is an interesting book. It is, I think, a sort of parable. The story is about a small seagull named Jonathan who wanted to do more than nibble on the tiny pieces of food he could find along the seashore. Jonathan wanted to fly more than anything else. He learned to do all kinds of maneuvers and aerodynamics as he continued to strive to become a great flyer. His parents did not understand his ambition and condemned his actions. For a while, Jonathan dropped back in step with all the other seagulls. But he could not stand that life for long. He wanted to fly faster than any seagull had ever been able to fly before.

Finally, one-day Jonathan succeeded and really did fly higher and faster than any other seagull, to his knowledge, had ever accomplished. When he landed after reaching his new goals, he told his fellow seagulls, "How much more there is now to living! Instead of drab slogging forth and back to the fishing boats, there's a deeper reason to life. We can lift ourselves out of ignorance, we can find ourselves as creatures of excellence and intelligence and skills. We can be free! We can learn to fly."[1]

Jonathan thought he would get an enthusiastic response from the other gulls for his accomplishments, but what he received from them was banishment and rejection. Nevertheless, he continued to fly at ten times the speed of most gulls and tried complicated dives and other feats of aerodynamics. While working on his flying techniques one day, he noticed that, although he was flying at an incredible speed, two celestial gulls that seemed to be glowing were at his wingtips. They led him into a further dimension of life. He thought he had been taken into heaven but discovered that wasn't true. Instead, it was another phase of continuing further into a new state of life and learning. He remained there for a while under the tutelage of a wise old gull until he felt a desire to return and share the good news he knew with the other gulls from where he had come.

Jonathan returned to earth and gathered a small group around him. Eventually he had twelve followers. One of his disciples hurt his wing, and Jonathan touched it with the tip of his own wing and healed him. Another gull ran into a mountain and was killed. Jonathan raised him from the dead. Then some of the gulls began to say, "This is the son of the great gull." But Jonathan rejected that notion and declared that he was free and could fly. "He spoke of very simple things—that it is right for a gull to fly, that whatever stands against that freedom must be set aside, be it ritual or superstition or limitation in any form."[2] He taught other gulls to learn to fly and love it. And the parable ended.

A Call to Be Different

This parable about Jonathan Livingston Seagull is probably a mixture of several perspectives. There is some Christianity rolled into this story, along with a dash of Hinduism, Buddhism, Christian Science, other religions, and maybe a little bit of Horatio Alger as well. One of the central thoughts in this parable is the quest to be perfect, to break free from one's limits, and to excel. I reflected on this parable as I struggled with Jesus' words, "Be perfect like your Father in heaven is perfect." Like the precepts of Jesus, this parable about a little seagull calls us to step out from the crowd and be different. Jonathan felt a call to be different from others and to seek to achieve what he thought was the highest purpose for his life. Jesus Christ, likewise, has called his disciples to a moral standard that is different from that of others. Conventional standards are not enough. Jesus lifts up a standard for the Christian that reaches far beyond simply being kind to other people, especially those who have been kind to us. Jesus' moral standard is a radical demand. The verses that precede our text indicate the radical nature of his call. Conventional responses will not fulfill this value system. Jesus states, "Do not swear at all. If someone compels you to go one mile, go two. If a person strikes you on one cheek, turn the other. If you are asked for your coat, give your topcoat as well" (Matt 5:33-42). These sayings are not reflective of conventional ethics. Christians are called to live a life that is radically different from the ways of the unchristian society where they walk daily.

This does not imply that Christians should seek to live by narrow restrictions or rigid confinements. Since our model for goodness comes from God, Christians seek in their friendships, kindnesses, and acts of love to be limitless and boundless like God. There should be no limits to our love, kindness, and friendships. We need to relate to others not as they have responded to us but as Christ would have us relate. We are not simply to give to others what they have given us; we are to respond as God has responded to us. *The New English Bible* translated the verse this way: "There must be no limit to your goodness, as your heavenly Father's goodness knows no bounds."

A Higher Standard

As Christians, we are called to a higher way, modeled after God. We are to imitate God. As Paul, writing to the Ephesians, says, "You have been created in Christ Jesus for good works" (Eph 2:10). We are to live a new lifestyle that we have seen in the life of Jesus Christ. This higher way is not limited to arbitrary restrictions or striving to be the champions of legalism. It is a call to live above the crowd's demands. Thoreau reminds us in *Walden*, "If a man [or woman] does not keep pace with his [or her] companions, perhaps it is because he [or she] hears a different drummer. Let him [or her] step to the music which one hears however measured or far way." The world often tries to force us into its role for morality. But Jesus Christ sounds a drumbeat that calls us to a higher standard. This radical call challenges us to love even as Christ has loved us. Unfortunately, the church often settles for the moral standards of the world instead of transforming the world. Christians have become conformed to the world, and the church's standards often exemplify or reflect the world's values instead of the values of Christ. I like the way *Phillips* translated Romans 12:2: "Don't let the world around you squeeze you into its own mold, but let God remold your minds from within, so you may prove in practice that the plan of God for you is good, meets all demands and moves toward the goal of true maturity."

One of my favorite parables from Søren Kierkegaard is the one where a wild goose flies down to a barnyard, where he sits on a fence and preaches to all the other geese living within it. The preaching goose tells the others about the world beyond the barnyard. He preaches about the wonder of the life they can have if they will use their wings and fly out of the barnyard. The geese applaud him, listening attentively, but do not respond. He flies away into the open sky and wider world. The others remain in the barnyard.

Jesus Christ has called us to a high standard that seems almost impossible to reach. Some of us refuse to try, but we are challenged to be good toward other people in the way that God is good toward us. We acknowledge that God loves us even when we are unlovable. God doesn't care for us just when we are good. God grants his goodness to people without discrimination. Even while we were sinners, Christ died for us. We need to fly out of the barnyard.

Not Remaining Content

This teaching from Jesus calls us to reach forward for our greatest growth, development, and potential and not be content with where we are. The little parable of Jonathan Livingston Seagull challenges the reader to strive to be more than he or she is. The parable from Kierkegaard calls the reader to escape narrow confines and reach his or her greater potential. Christ calls each of us to reach for the highest within ourselves. In Greek, the word for perfect can mean end, aim, or goal. The perfection it describes is functional. It doesn't mean flawlessness. The aim is to fulfill the purpose for which something was created. One can have a perfect hammer when that hammer drives nails properly. One can have a perfect saw when that saw fulfills its function to cut wood properly. One can have a perfect piano when the piano is able to fulfill its purpose and serve as an instrument on which a good melody, hymn, or song can be played. A typewriter fulfills its perfect function when it is used to produce a typed letter or book. Our lives can be perfect when they fulfill what God has created us to be. We have been created in God's image; therefore, God motivates us never to be content with what we have become or who we are, but to reach even higher, to be like God. We are to pattern ourselves after God.

The Challenge of Perfection

The challenge to be perfect is a constant reminder that we cannot be content with where we have arrived in our spiritual journey. The Christian is not to feel trapped or confined by his or her limitations. The call to perfection constantly pulls us forward. All of our lives, we will feel this tug upward. The way is not easy, but the call is to continue forward. Browning expressed that truth in this line: "a man's reach must exceed his grasp / Or what's a heaven for?" (in his poem *Andrea del Sarto*). William James has reminded us, "In any project, the important factor is your belief. Without belief, there can be no successful outcome. That is fundamental." If we are to succeed at anything, every one of us must believe that what we are trying to accomplish can be realized. Too many people do not have enough faith in themselves and in what they can do individually. They simply give up and do not try at all.

I love the story about the time the New York Yankees and the Chicago White Sox were in a World Series baseball game. Babe Ruth was at the height of his career. The White Sox were leading four to three in the fifth inning. Babe Ruth had already hit one home run, so Charlie Root, the pitcher, was not too concerned when he came to the plate. After one home run, he thought it was unlikely that Babe Ruth could hit another that day. He threw a fastball across the plate, and Ruth stepped back and held up one finger in derision to indicate strike one. The second pitch went across the plate and Ruth held up the second finger to note strike two. Then Ruth stepped back from the plate and pointed to the fence where he intended to hit the ball. Sure enough, Root threw the ball straight across the plate. Ruth hit the ball with a loud crack and it arched high in the air, sailing right over the fence where he had pointed. After the game, someone asked

Ruth, "Suppose you had missed that final strike?" Ruth looked back in a rather surprised manner and responded, "Why, I never even thought of such a thing!"

Often, we are not able to reach certain goals because we have no faith in our own gifts to accomplish them, and consequently we make no effort to realize them. We focus instead on our failures, weaknesses, limitations, and restrictions and do not see the potential and the possibilities that lie before us.

Our Efforts Are Not Enough

Having made that point, let me offer a warning. For me, one of the big problems with the parable of Jonathan Livingston Seagull is that the writer seems to call the reader to a will to power. That is, he implies that we accomplish whatever we want to do in life by our own strength. This philosophy asserts that we can execute whatever we wish on our own initiative. If we simply try hard enough, we can do anything. I do not believe a person can reach the moral standards to which God has called us simply by sheer effort or willpower. In an article in *Theology Today*, written about *Jonathan Livingston Seagull*, the writer, John W. Kuykendall, observed,

> The point is that the book espouses the quest for perfection as the absolute goal of life. Limitless freedom is the meaning of heaven. Jon is not the Son of the Great Gull; he is simply the model or example of perfect freedom. He is the one from whom all the other gulls who read the book can draw the incentive to go and do likewise. The ring of pelagian knowledge is complete: *You can because you know you can*.[3]

Herein lies the real weakness of Richard Bach's story: there are limitations in all of our lives. Our sin burdens us. Jesus reminds us that we are able to live by his standard only by the grace of God. The new birth experience in Christ opens the door to an authentic relationship with God. Jesus said, "Be perfect as your Father is perfect." Here is the key: our link is God. Like father like son. Like father like daughter. We can find strength to live this kind of life because we are linked to God the Father. "I can do all things through Christ who strengthens me," Paul wrote (Phil 4:13).

We live and love like our God. God defines our way, and we imitate God. We are not just nice people but new creations. We live the Christian life not by our own efforts but by the power of God. Linking my life with God, I seek to follow God's way. My relationship to God makes it possible for me to live in a radically different way. We are what we are not by works but by grace. Our moral living comes about from the strength we draw from God. It is realized not by our strength alone but by the strength we receive as we are linked with the strength of God. God's presence fortifies us to live morally. These seemingly impossible demands, when linked with God, are possible. We discover that we are able to be people who live high moral lives with values that seem greater than we could ever imagine because we draw strength directly from God. This difficult saying from Jesus challenges us not to limit our goodness but to model our behavior after the goodness of God, which has no bounds.

Seeking a Higher Vision

We are called by our text to a higher vision of what we can be as people. As the Scriptures have said, "Without a vision the people perish" (Prov 29:18). Sometimes individuals and churches lose their vision of what they can be. I heard about a woman who was going to see her psychiatrist. She told a friend, "I haven't had any dreams lately that my psychiatrist and I can talk about. Lend me one of your dreams." What kind of help do you get by borrowing somebody else's dream? Too many people have lost their dreams and visions and live off somebody else's. Individuals who have made a radical difference in the world have held on to their dreams, visions, and new possibilities.

Vision Inspires Creativity

Creativity is born out of vision. What would the world be without vision? Everything that has come into existence has happened because somebody had a dream or a vision. Columbus had a dream of a new world. Galileo had a vision of a new scientific approach. Edison had a dream that sound could travel over a wire and that electricity could produce light. Ford had a vision of a horseless carriage. The Wright brothers dreamed that people could fly. Von Braun dreamed that human beings could go to the moon and beyond.

What would religion be without vision? Abraham followed his vision of God and went looking for a city without foundations. Moses saw God in a burning bush. Jacob wrestled with God at Peniel. Ezekiel had a vision of God at Chebar. Isaiah had a vision of God high and lifted up in the temple. Elijah experienced God in a sound of gentle stillness in a mountain cave. Paul had a life-changing vision of Christ on the Damascus Road. Augustine had a vision of the "city of God." Luther had a vision of a reformed church.

Wesley had a vision of a church in revival. Albert Schweitzer had a vision of reverence for all of life. Martin Luther King, Jr., had a dream that all men and women could be brothers and sisters together. Mother Teresa had a vision of the church's concern for the poor and outcast of society.

What would the church be without vision? Without vision, the church would cease to exist. Only when men and women dream dreams, see visions, formulate plans, and prophesy do we see real living. Christ has summoned us from complacency to adventure; from apathy to enthusiasm; from the settled to the pioneer; from safety to risk; from comfort to danger; from death to life. Hang on to the vision that God holds before you.

Do not be content with less. We are challenged to reach toward what God wants us to be. God calls us to be perfect. Perfection is always an ever-receding goal. When we reach toward God to grow spiritually, we realize how much greater God is and how sinful we are. But we continually model our lives after God and strive to be nurtured by God's grace and love. We may never arrive, but we continue to reach for the goal.

One of the images of the church in the New Testament is a ship. You may have heard some of the commercials for the Kentucky Derby and the great steamboat race in Louisville. In a commercial for the Kingfish restaurant, one of the boats in the steamboat race is anchored in concrete. I have thought that this picture, unfortunately, describes the church. The church, which is supposed to be a ship for God, is often anchored in concrete. It is unable to move into the world to touch human lives and bring them the transforming love of God. God has called his church to set sail and go into the world and change it. We are to be the salt, light, and leaven.

One of my favorite songs comes from the musical *The Man of La Mancha*. This powerful song summons us to reach for "the unreachable star" as we encounter all kinds of struggles and sorrows—and move forward without question or pause, even going into hell itself for a heavenly cause until one lies down for rest from this glorious quest. The concluding lines attest our assurance of the rightfulness of our cause:

> And the world will be better for this
> That one man, scorned and covered with scars
> Still strove with his last ounce of courage
> To reach the unreachable star.[4]

In our text, Jesus Christ challenges us to imitate God. We are to link our lives with God and let our goodness exemplify the boundless goodness we have experienced in God. God has not lowered God's standards and made it easy for us to accomplish this goal. Jesus has lifted before us a goal that seems impossible. But our Lord is beside us to guide us, undergird us, and help us live the Christ-like life. May God grant that we will seek to continue to follow, no matter how hard or difficult the way.

Notes

1. Richard Bach, *Jonathan Livingston Seagull* (New York: Avon Books, 1970) 30–31.

2. Ibid., 114.

3. John W. Kuykendall, "Sinners and Seagulls: Pelagius Redux," *Theology Today*, July 1973, p. 183.

4. "The Impossible Dream," *The Man of La Mancha*, lyrics by Joe Darion, music by Mitch Leigh, Cherry Lane Music, Greenwich CT, 1965.

14

The Jot and Tittle of Religion

Matthew 5:17-21

In our text, Jesus says something that must have astonished his original listeners: "I have come not to destroy the Law, but to fulfill it, and not a jot or a tittle of it will disappear until all has been accomplished." These words continue to be perplexing to those of us who read the Gospels seriously today. This is a difficult saying from Jesus. Why? First, Jesus' own words in other places seem to contradict this statement. He violated many of the laws and traditions of the scribes and Pharisees. He did not ask his disciples to observe the ritual of hand-washing before eating. He broke the Sabbath laws by healing on the Sabbath. His disciples plucked grain as they went through a field on the Sabbath, which was considered working. In fact, Jesus was crucified because he was considered a lawbreaker! Since Jesus broke many of these laws, it sounds strange that he should instruct others to keep all of the laws. It is indeed a rather amazing statement.

Second, this statement seems to conflict with what the Apostle Paul wrote in his epistles. In Romans 10:4 Paul wrote that "Christ is the end of the law." He stated that Jesus "abolished in flesh the law with its commandments and ordinances" (Eph 2:15). The Law, Paul stated, "once held us captive" but now "we are discharged from the law" (Rom 7:6). The Law had been seen as a schoolteacher (Gal 3:24) that led people to Christ. But now we are free from the demands of the Law. "For by grace are you saved through faith," Paul wrote, "not by works lest any persons should boast" (Eph 2:8). Grace set the Law aside. William Barclay, in his commentary on Romans, wrote,

Jesus Christ is the end of the law. . . . The relationship between God and man is no longer the relationship between a creditor and a debtor; between an earner and accessor; between a judge and a man standing at the bar of judgment. Because Jesus Christ lived and brought His message to men, man is no longer faced with the task of satisfying God's justice; he can only accept God's love. He has no longer to win God's favor; he has to take the grace and love and mercy which God freely offers to him.[1]

Don't Minimize the Less Significant Aspect of the Law

What are we to make of this statement by Jesus in light of his violations of some of the laws and the words of the Apostle Paul? Jesus says, "not one jot or tittle will pass away." Jot is the Hebrew word *Yod*, the smallest letter of the Hebrew alphabet. The "tittle" or "dot" was a small mark or a little flourish on a letter to distinguish it from another letter. You and I might express this same image today that it is like the "dotting of an 'i' or the crossing of a 't.'" Jesus was saying that even the most insignificant aspect of the Law must not be disregarded.

Defining the Law

What is the Law? The Jewish people gave various interpretations in defining the Law. To some, the Law constituted the Ten Commandments. To others, the Law was the first five books or scrolls of the Old Testament, the Pentateuch. To others, the Law and the Prophets constituted the whole of the Old Testament. Still others believed that the oral or scribal traditions were the Law. By the middle of the third century, these rabbinical traditions were compiled into a book called the Mishnah. Later rabbinical scholars made commentaries on the Mishnah called the Talmud. There are twelve volumes of the Jerusalem Talmud and sixty commentaries of the Talmud in the Babylonian church. As you can see, there were various interpretations on what constituted the Law itself. But for strict Jews who wanted to be orthodox, there were literally thousands of rules and regulations to follow.

Not Jesus' Words?

Some scholars face this problematic text by saying that they do not believe Jesus spoke these words. They see them as a later addition by Christian Jews who wanted to keep the Law central in the faith. Since Matthew was written originally for Jews, this was to help them see that our Lord wanted his followers to abide by the Torah. Other New Testament scholars, like

T. W. Manson, believe that the words in our text should be understood from the perspective of "bitter irony." Rather than a dogmatic statement, Jesus meant the opposite of what he said. Speaking to the scribes and Pharisees, Manson paraphrases Jesus saying, "The world will come to an end before you give up the tiniest part of your traditional interpretation of the Law."[2]

An Eternal Validity to the Moral Law

That is a possible interpretation, but after researching this text I personally believe that Jesus meant what he said. Let me share with you what I think Jesus means by this difficult passage. *First, he is saying that there is an eternal validity to the moral law of God.* Jesus is not attempting to invalidate the Law. He never hesitated to break the traditions, customs, or ceremonial/judiciary laws of the scribes and Pharisees. Jesus did not see these laws as the moral law of God. The moral law is seen in the Ten Commandments. The Ten Commandments are as true today as they were when God delivered them to Moses. We still should not kill or commit adultery. These laws continue to be valid. There is continuity between the new teachings of Jesus and the old. When Jesus gave a summary of the Law, he said, "You are to love the Lord your God with all your heart, with all your soul, and with all your strength, and with your entire mind" (Matt 22:37). This is the Shema that Jewish people recite every day. Then Jesus added, "And you shall love your neighbor as yourself." In another summary of the law, Jesus gave us the Golden Rule: "Do unto others as you would have them do unto you, for this is the Law and the prophets" (Matt 7:12). The moral law within the universe abides, no matter how much change happens around us. This moral law remains absolute.

Although we may be Christians and live under grace, this does not mean that the moral laws have been set aside and we are free to do anything we desire. Paul faced this argument with some of the early Christians. They thought that since they were under grace, they no longer had to abide by the moral law. "The moral laws of God continue," Paul argued.

I read about a man who went to a store and got a shortwave radio but refused to take out a license. He was arrested and brought before the judge. In his defense, he said that the set was not really his but he had gotten it from the dealer "on approval." Until he decided to buy it, he did not think he was obligated to get a license. But the judge ruled this way: "The law knows nothing about 'approval.' The law is to be obeyed. Pay the fine."

The eternal moral law of God is absolute. Jesus Christ was in no way attempting to abolish it. We are to abide by it.

The Purpose behind the Law

Second, Jesus wanted us to learn that the best way to keep a commandment is to see the purpose behind the moral law. Jesus did not hesitate to break some of the ceremonial or scribal traditions. He didn't consider these rules a part of God's eternal law. Even the fourth commandment about keeping the Sabbath day holy had to be understood in light of the purpose behind the commandment. What did it mean not to do any work on the Sabbath? Rabbinical laws carefully defined "work" on the Sabbath. They drew up a long list of rules and descriptions about work; for example, a woman sticking a needle in a dress was bearing a burden, thus working. Their laws forbade providing healing to anybody on the Sabbath. They would not let someone die if they could possibly help, but they would only permit efforts to get a person to a point where he or she would be stable. Then, the next day they could try to bring healing to the person. Jesus said, "That's nonsense." We have to see the purpose behind the Sabbath laws. The Sabbath was created for the sake of people; people were not created for the Sabbath. The purpose of the Sabbath is to bring rest and relief. Anything that assists in that end is permitted. Jesus, therefore, felt that it was appropriate to heal on the Sabbath because it was not only proper but also honored the Creator's purpose for the Sabbath. Jesus' emphasis was on life, not on the letter of the law.

Reverence for God

The real purpose behind the moral law of God is that we might have reverence for God, for God's name, and for the Sabbath. We are to respect other people, including their rights, reputation, prerogatives, and property. Jesus is not attempting to abolish all of the abiding moral law but is calling us to learn how to live and respond to the God who is behind it. He is not trying to bind more heavy burdens on our backs by giving us restrictive rules and regulations; instead, he wants us to worship and obey the God who established the law in the first place.

If I go into a store and buy a suit, I can pay for the suit and my obligation to the seller will be completed. I do not owe him anything else once I have paid. But that is not true of my parents. They gave me my life and so much more through their love and guidance when I was a child. My obligation to them cannot be satisfied. It is an unpayable debt. So it is with our obligation to God. We cannot satisfy our debt to God. The moral law of God is constant. It helps us see our responsibility to the God who created life and how we can relate to this God and our fellow human beings.

The Right Motive

Third, Jesus states that the keeping of the Law begins with the right motive within a person's heart. Any overt action stems from a thought from within. Out of the heart come the issues of life. What is within your mind determines how you relate to others. In Matthew 5:21-48, Jesus gives six illustrations about the motives behind our actions. He begins with murder. He says, "Murder is not confined to killing somebody physically. Murder begins with an attitude of hatred within one's mind. Adultery is not limited to the physical act. Adultery begins with lust in a person's mind or heart." Jesus also speaks about oath taking, overcoming evil with good, and loving your enemy as illustrations or examples that focus on the motive behind such actions. The key to keeping the Law lies within. Examine your intention, your attitude, and your motive.

Jesus Came to Complete the Law

Fourth, Jesus said that he came to fulfill the Law, not to abolish it. If Jesus had come to destroy the Law, he would have been a revolutionary. But Jesus said, "I have not come to set aside the Law, the moral law of God. I have come to make its meaning full or complete." Rather than destroying the Law, Jesus extends it further. "In Jesus there has come true what the Law and the prophets only announced," Eduard Schweizer noted. "In him has come the fullness that was intended in them but not attained."[3] What the Law stated was good, but it did not reach deep enough into the reason behind a person's action. Jesus fulfilled the Law with his more expanded teaching. In itself, the Law was incomplete. It was completed—fulfilled—in Christ's life and teachings. Jesus did not set aside the Law, but he expanded it so people could understand more fully how God wants them to feel in their hearts, think with their minds, or use their strength. Jesus did indeed fulfill the Law and the prophecy.

Old Testament prophecy told about where Jesus would be born, the kind of life he would live, and the death he would die—even the fact that Gentiles would one day come into God's grace. Jesus said, "I have come to fulfill, complete, and satisfy all of these laws." What an amazing statement that is! The New Testament affirms this truth on almost all its pages.

The problem with first-century Judaism is that its people became so entangled within its laws and traditions that they thought they had God captured in the Law. If a person kept the Law, then somehow or another that person could fully satisfy God's will. Some of the early the disciples of Jesus thought they didn't need any laws. Grace, they believed, made them completely free from these laws. Confronting these two extreme attitudes, Jesus, according to Dietrich Bonhoeffer, vindicates the divine authority of the Law:

> God is the giver and its Lord, and only in personal communion with God is the law fulfilled. There is no fulfillment of the law apart from communion with God, and no communion with God apart from fulfillment of the law. To forget the first condition was the mistake of the Jews, and to forget the second the temptation of the disciples. Jesus, the Son of God, who alone lives *in* perfect communion with *him*, vindicates the law of the old Covenant by coming to fulfill it. He was the only man who ever fulfilled the law, and therefore he alone can teach the law and fulfillment aright.[4]

The moral law of God continues. It is constant. We seek to follow the Christ who alone fulfills and completed that Law. Only he was completely sinless. He fulfilled the will of God in his life, teaching, and death. He alone realized fully in his commitment to his Father the deepest meaning within and behind the Law.

A Call to a Higher Righteousness

Finally, note that the Law, through Jesus' interpretation, calls us to a higher righteousness as we are obedient to him. He says that a believer's righteousness should go beyond the righteousness of the scribes and Pharisees. This shows how seriously Jesus takes moral living. You can't say you are a Christian and live any way you want to. You can't say you are a Christian, a disciple of Jesus Christ, and live a scandalous life and cast aside all the laws about murder, adultery, and other sins. Jesus calls his disciples to the highest standards of moral living. He says that our righteousness has to exceed that of the scribes and Pharisees. Unfortunately, many of us have been taught that the scribes and Pharisees were bad people. One Sunday school teacher warned her pupils one day, "Now let's not be like this nasty old Pharisee." However, the Pharisees were not seen as evil people by the Jews; they were considered some of the most moral people in Israel. The scribes were the ones who interpreted the laws and kept the records of traditions. The Pharisees were the separate ones who attempted literally to live by these laws. They sought to follow them to the minutest detail.

In the fourth book of Maccabees, one of the interbiblical books, there is the story about a priest named Eleazar who is brought before Antiochus Epiphanes, the emperor of Babylon. The emperor is trying to stamp out the Jewish religion. Antiochus orders Eleazar to eat pork, which is against his Jewish faith, or he will put him to death. Eleazar refuses. He is then beaten severely. But he continues to maintain that it is against the Law of God. Some of the soldiers feel sorry for him and offer him some other kind of meat, saying that they will pretend it is pork. But Eleazar still refuses to eat the meat. Finally, he is put to death because he will not comply.

Think about that. This is the kind of devotion some Jewish people had to the Law. You and I might say this was a mistaken devotion, but to them there was a great identity of the Law with God. Often the Jewish people identified their traditions and external customs too much with the Law itself. They were not able to see the significance of the motive behind the Law. They seldom made a distinction between a person's action and the cause of the action. The Pharisees often made themselves an exception to their own rules. This is the reason Jesus called them hypocrites. Jesus called his disciples to a righteousness that went beyond that of the Pharisees. But that is almost like telling an amateur golfer that he or she has to play better than a professional. The professional holy people were the scribes and Pharisees, and the Christian is challenged to live a life of righteousness greater than theirs. Jesus' disciples are to live a life that is purer, more spotless, and more righteous than the lives of these "holy" people.

Jesus is not trying to teach a righteousness by works. He is not telling us that, though the Pharisees fail by their attempt to fulfill the Law, you and I have to fulfill it in another way. We are still saved by grace. But as James says, "Faith without works is dead" (Jas 2:17). Jesus is saying that any person who is his disciple will be known by his or her fruits. People will see that we are disciples of Jesus by the way we live. We now walk not according to the flesh but according to the Spirit. This will not be easy. It will take complete commitment to Christ and his way. We will need his grace for strength to live such a life.

Many years ago in Sweden, a visitor went to a church one day and noticed a beautiful crucifix on the wall opposite the pulpit. He wondered why it was opposite the pulpit instead of in front of the church where all the people could see it. This was the story: One day when the pastor was getting up to preach his sermon, the king of Sweden came into the service.

When the minister saw the king, he changed his sermon and eulogized the king for his virtues. That week the king sent the pastor this crucifix and instructed that it be placed opposite the pulpit so that no matter who was in the congregation, the preacher would see it and remember what he was supposed to preach.

The Law calls us to focus on God. The cross of Jesus Christ reveals his willingness to follow the will of God in his teaching, living, and death. His commitment fulfilled the will of God. He has called us to walk in the way that is beyond ordinary living. This way will not be easy, but it leads to abundant life. Every time we come to the Communion Table, we are reminded of the cross of Christ and the One who laid down his life for us in obedience to his Father. As we partake of the bread and the cup, we do so as a sign of taking Christ into our lives, accepting his saving grace, renewing our commitment to obey his moral teachings, and following in the steps of the Christ who is the Lord of all life.

Notes

1. William Barclay, *The Letter to the Romans* (Philadelphia: Westminster Press, 1957) 147.

2. T. W. Manson, *The Sayings of Jesus* (London: SCM Press, 1949) 135.

3. Eduard Schweizer, *The Good News According to Matthew* (Atlanta: John Knox Press, 1977) 107.

4. Dietrich Bonhoeffer, *The Cost of Discipleship* (London: SCM Press, 1959) 111.

15

How Can Jesus Be the Resurrection and the Life?

John 11:17-44

The head gravedigger was a squat, square-jawed, muscular old man, and he commanded the other gravediggers like a staff sergeant. Homer McEwen was conducting his first funeral at Southview Cemetery in Atlanta, Georgia. He had arrived a little early and was waiting for the pallbearers to get there. The head gravedigger walked over to him and said, "You must be a new preacher around here. These Atlanta preachers don't come to the cemetery 'less it's some big shot or somebody what left them some money." "Since everybody gets just as dead as the next fellow," the preacher responded, "I come with every bereaved family. Why should we desert the mourners at the time of the burial?" "Well," the gravedigger went on, "I don't see what good all this does nohow. Men like you keep comin' out here talkin' about 'a sure and certain hope of the resurrection through Jesus Christ.' Everyone of 'em is gonna die. And preacher, there will be a hole for you, either here or someplace else." "Yes," the minister admitted, "but when that time comes God will have another minister standing at my graveside repeating that same hope and promise over me. And so it will be as long as the race survives." For a moment, the gravedigger grew silent. Then, with a smile he said, "Now, that's somethin' for me to ponder. Never thought about it like that before. But, preacher, dead is dead. Besides, you ain't talkin' about nuthin' you can prove."[1]

Another Cemetery

Put that story on hold for a few moments. We will come back to the gravedigger. Go with me now to another cemetery. The setting is two thousand years ago. Jesus had gone on a trip toward Jericho. He received word from his good friends in Bethany that Lazarus, the brother of Mary and Martha, was gravely ill. The sisters wanted Jesus to come immediately to Bethany. They thought he might be able to do something to help their brother. It probably took the messenger a whole day to reach Jesus from Bethany. But Jesus delayed four days before he went to his friends. When he arrived, Lazarus had been dead for four days.

Bethany was a small hillside village that was only about two miles from Jerusalem. Jesus often found refuge from the crowd at the home of Mary, Martha, and Lazarus—a place to eat, sleep, and converse. They were his good friends. But for some reason Jesus delayed getting to Bethany. The two women probably looked longingly down the road daily, waiting for Jesus. When he finally arrived, Martha met him and exclaimed, "Lord, if you had only been here my brother might not have died." Mary stated the same thing later: "If only you had been here!"

Lord, why did you delay? Most of us have at some point felt that God was delayed in coming to us. We have experienced times when we prayed to God to give us some kind of response in times of need, and there seemed to be none. You are sick in the hospital and you pray for relief, but you do not receive it. God seems to be delayed. You lose your job, and you pray for guidance and help. God seems to be delayed and nowhere to be found. Your son or daughter is killed in an automobile accident, and you cry out and ask, "God, where are you?" There are moments in our lives when we experience illness, grief, death, loneliness, or depression and wonder where God is. God seems so remote, distant, and delayed in answering our plea. Why doesn't God come? Why does God seem to linger somewhere else? We understand Mary and Martha's question.

Jesus turned to Martha and said, "I am the resurrection and the life. Whosoever believes in me, even if he dies, will live again. And anyone who is alive and believes in me shall *never* die. Do you believe this?" What a question at a time like that! But Martha responded with one of the highest confessions of faith in all the Scriptures: "Yes, Lord, I believe that you are the Messiah, the son of the living God, the one who was to come into the world." Her statement of faith was based on her personal acquaintance with the one who was "the resurrection and the life."

Jesus at the Center of His Teachings

Jesus said, "I am the resurrection and the life." Jesus said, "*I*," not some abstract thoughts about himself, not some doctrinal or philosophical systems or beliefs about himself. Jesus put himself at the center of his teachings. "If *I* be lifted up, *I* will draw all men unto me." "*I* am the way the truth and the life." "*I* am the Good Shepherd." "*I* am the Vine." "*I* am the Bread of Life." "*I* am the resurrection and the life." Jesus put himself at the forefront of his teaching, and we need to respond to him because he is the avenue, the pathway, the medium that leads us to God. The ethical and moral teachings of Jesus are important, and they reflect who he was.

Albert Einstein came to the United States as a refugee from Germany. He was banished from Germany because he was Jewish. In an interview in America, his wife was once asked, "Do you understand all about your husband's theory of relativity?" She smiled and responded, "No, but I know my husband."

Who understands all the doctrines of the faith? Who understands all about the mystery of the incarnation or the atonement or life after death? Who understands everything about the teachings in the Bible? None of us. But we are drawn to Jesus Christ because he is the one who reveals God to us. The "I" calls for a response from each of us. Brian McLaren declares, "We must understand the essence of faith to be something other than a list of opinions, propositions, or statements that our group holds but cannot prove."[2] Our focus is on Jesus and his way of sacrificial love.

A Present Possession

Jesus said, "I *am*." The life he was giving was not something off in the future. The life that Jesus gives is a present possession. This life is something we have in the present moment. As John says, "This *is* eternal life, that they may know you, the only real God, and Jesus Christ whom you have sent" (John 17:3). To be in Christ is to have eternal life. The emphasis is on "I *am*."

I'm sure you have seen signs that read, "Prepare for eternity" or "Are you ready for eternity?" Jesus is telling us that eternal life is something that is present; it is not confined to the future or something that comes after this life. "This is eternal life," John says, "to know the Son." Eternal life is a present possession. It is something that you and I have in this moment. It is not some reward we get in the future after death. The eternal life that Christ gives begins today.

Two sailors were set adrift in the ocean after their boat sank. They floated for days in their small craft and almost died of thirst. Finally, they saw another ship and were rescued. The first thing they begged for was water. But the sailors on the rescuing ship said, "Let down your buckets. You are a mile into the Amazon River. You are not in the ocean and the water is fresh here."

Let down your buckets into the grace of God's love that surrounds you everywhere. Let down the bucket of your life and drink of the presence of God that is available now. Eternal life is not something we receive after death. This is eternal life: to know the Son now.

Jesus as the Resurrection

"I am the *resurrection*," Jesus said. "Do you believe this?" he asked Martha. Do you think she began to comprehend the real meaning of the resurrection in that moment? No, not really. Even her high confession did not reveal that kind of knowledge. The disciples had not grasped it either. "I am the resurrection." What a claim! Look at Jesus' disciples after the crucifixion as they gathered in the upper room, frightened that they, too, would be put to death like their Lord. They were dejected and in despair. The one that they had hoped was the promised Messiah was crucified. They were ashamed because they had fled and not stayed with him during his ordeal on the cross. All of their hopes, all of their dreams, all that they had longed for seemed gone. And so they gathered in that small room, feeling only despair and hopelessness. But when the risen Lord appeared, they were radically transformed. The resurrection of Jesus Christ is the foundation of the church. It made all the difference in the lives of the disciples. It filled their preaching and writings. "I am the resurrection."

The Centrality of the Resurrection in the New Testament

Several verses in the book of Acts affirm the importance of the resurrection: "With great power the apostles gave witness of the resurrection of the Lord Jesus; and great grace was upon them all" (4:33). "Paul preached Jesus and the resurrection" (17:8). "At Athens when they heard of the resurrection of the dead, some mocked" (17:32). "Before Felix Paul preached the resurrection both of the just and the unjust" (24:15). Then, writing to the Corinthian church, Paul said, "If Christ has not been raised, then our preaching is in vain. Your faith is also in vain. . . . You are still in your sins. If in this life only we have hope in Christ, we of all persons are most pitiful, but now Christ has been raised from the dead" (1 Cor 15:14-20). And, in the letter to the Ephesians he said he was writing "that you may know the exceeding greatness of his power to us who believe according to the working strength of his might which he wrought in Christ, when he raised him from the dead, and made him to sit at the right hand of the heavenly Father" (Eph 1:18-21). To the Philippians, he said he wanted to "know the power of his resurrection" (Phil 3:10). In Hebrews, the writer said that Jesus "ever lives to make intercession for us" (Heb 7:25). In 1 Peter the writer proclaimed, "Blessed be the God and Father of our Lord Jesus Christ, who according to his great mercy begat us again unto a living hope by the resurrection of Jesus Christ from the dead" (1:3). Then, in Revelation, John said, "Behold, cries the risen Christ, I am alive for evermore and I have the keys of death and of Hades" (1:18).

The resurrection was at the center of the early church's teachings. Because Jesus proclaimed, "I am the resurrection," and rose from the grave, the church acknowledges the resurrected Lord as the reason we celebrate Easter today. Jesus Christ offers a radical difference in the newness of real life. The resurrection life he offers can come from no other.

A noted preacher in Birmingham, England, R. W. Dale, was preparing his Easter sermon some years ago. In the midst of the preparation for that sermon, it suddenly hit him what it meant to talk about the risen Christ. He began to say to himself, "Christ is alive, alive." Then he paused and said again, "Alive. Alive? Can that really be true? Living as really I myself am." He got up from his desk and walked around repeating, "Christ is living! Christ is living!" "At first," he later wrote, "it seemed strange and hardly true. But at last it came upon me as a burst of certain glory. Yes, Christ is alive. It was to me a new discovery. I thought that all along I had believed but not until that moment did I feel sure about it. I then said, 'My people shall know it and I shall preach it again and again until they believe it as I do now.'"[3]

Life in Christ

"I am the resurrection and the *life*," Jesus said. "Life" is one of John's favorite words in his Gospel. He uses it more than thirty-three times. Life in some ways is larger than the word "resurrection" because resurrection comes out of the life of God. This is eternal *life*: to know the Son. Jesus offers the believer resurrection and life today.

It is amazing how many people do not have real life. The poet Rilke captures this truth in his refrain: "The deadliest death of all is to be alive and not know it." There is life that God offers to us. But look around at people and see how many of them do not have this life. Many people exist but do not live. They look but they do not see. They reach out to touch but they do not feel. They speak but they do not communicate. They listen but they do not hear. They taste but they do not savor. Many of us look past each other, through each other, or around each other. We go through life as dead people, not really enjoying all the radiance of the life that God gives to us. We are pulled in so many directions. Life is spent rushing from one arena to another, hoping to find meaning.

The *Peanuts* comic strip shows Sally talking to Charlie Brown one morning. "My alarm clock didn't go off," Sally observes. "Maybe I wound it up too tight. Sometimes if you wind an alarm clock too tight, it won't go off." "We are all a little that way, aren't we?" Charlie Brown notes.

A lot of us get wound too tight. We are wound up to the point that we become broken, fragmented, burned out, and exhausted. We are living but not alive. Each day is greeted with uncertainty, boredom, apathy, fear, or dread. Some of us go through life, but little of life moves through us. Life is empty, routine, and meaningless. We are "living" as dead people. Jesus has come to give us life. Will we receive it?

Emotions Jesus Expressed at Lazarus's Grave

Jesus asked Martha to walk with him to the grave where Lazarus was buried. As they walked, Jesus began to grow angry. The Greek word for anger is "to snort" like a horse. What caused his anger? Was he angry with the people who were unbelievers? Was he angry about the powers of death that had snatched away the life of Lazarus? We don't know. In the shortest verse in the New Testament, it says that "Jesus wept." Did Jesus weep because of the death of his friend, Lazarus? Did these tears reveal his humanity? Did he weep because of the unwillingness or lack of understanding of people in recognizing who he was? Did he weep because he knew what glory he was bringing Lazarus back from? We do not know for sure.

A Denial of Death

Death is a reality that so many of us do not want to face, admit, or acknowledge. We often do everything we can to avoid the subject of death. We usually do not even think about death until we get past twenty-five. In the small book *Children's Letters to God,* a lad writes, "Dear God, what is it like when you die? Nobody will tell me. I just want to know, I don't want to do it. Your friend. Signed, Mike."[4] Dear God, what is it like to die? We all want to know the answer to that child's question. Indeed, we do. But most of us are terrified at the thought of death.

Rolling Away the Stone on the Grave

Jesus said, "Roll the stone away." The huge stone was shaped like an oxcart wheel and rolled in a small trench in front of the cave to secure the tomb. Martha protested, "But Lord, he has been dead four days. He will have begun to stink by now." Jesus told them, "You will see the glory of God." After praying, he cried, "Lazarus, come forth!" And the dead man came out from the tomb. Someone has said that there is a startling truth here about Jesus. Jesus had a voice that woke the dead. "Lazarus, come forth!"

Many are buried in some kind of tomb of their own. They are virtually dead to life. They may be in tombs of addiction, guilt, fear, anxieties, depression, unbelief, doubt, lust, or some secret sin. They may be buried in all kinds of tombs. If you are buried in such a tomb, let Christ call you out of it. Jesus stands before you and cries, "Come forth. Find life. I am the resurrection and the life." Jesus has come to give you real meaning and purpose. Why stay buried in your tomb when Jesus has come to set you free?

Lazarus's Experience in the Grave

Have you ever wondered what Lazarus experienced during those four days in the grave? Various writers have pondered near-death experiences that some people have had.[5] I wonder what Lazarus told his friends and family.

Eugene O'Neill wrote a play titled *Lazarus Laughed*. This play begins with Lazarus being raised dramatically by Jesus from the grave. Lazarus's friends ask him, "What did you experience? What was it like? What happened?" Friends and family gather for a meal together, and the father of Lazarus proposes a toast. "A toast to my son Lazarus, whom a blessed miracle has brought back from death." But Lazarus, speaking in a voice like a loving whisper of hope and confidence, says, "No, there is no death." People all around began to ask, "There is no death?" Lazarus laughs. He says in exultation, "There is only life. I heard the heart of Jesus laughing in my heart and it said there is Eternal life in No, and there is the same Eternal life in Yes! Death is the fear between! And my heart reborn to love of life cried, 'Yes!' and I laughed in the laughter of God!"

Lazarus begins to laugh, and he laughs and laughs, and all the others join him in laughter. Then Lazarus says, "Laugh! Laugh with me! Death is dead! Fear is no more! There is only life! There is only laughter!"[6]

"I am the resurrection and the life," Jesus said. Let's return now to the gravedigger story. The preacher went back to the cemetery a few months later for another funeral. He found shelter under a canopy to avoid the rain. There under the canopy was the same old gravedigger. "Preacher," the gravedigger asked, "do you still believe what you say over the dead?" The preacher replied, "I certainly do; otherwise I would not say it." "Do you believe like this all the time?" the gravedigger wondered. "The circumstances of life drive me occasionally to despair and doubt," the minister acknowledged. "But like one who finds the sunlight more brilliant because he has looked at darkness for a season, I turn again to the light of faith." The old gravedigger put his calloused hands on the preacher's shoulder and said, "That's a good way to be, a good way. Especially when you're like me, with so little time to go."[7]

On Easter Sunday or any other day, let's confess that no one has all the answers about life and death. But we can affirm that we know Jesus Christ as Lord, and because he lives, we too can live. Jesus said, "I am the resurrection and the life. Whosoever believes in me, even if he dies, will live again. And anyone who is alive and believes in me shall never die." Do you believe this?

Joyce Rupp has offered this prayer of assurance:

Risen Christ, we turn to you with full reliance on your resurrected presence with us here and now. We renew our trust in your grace to restore our joy when it lies hidden in our entombed self. Turn us again and again toward hope. Open our heart to recognize you in the garden of our everyday lives. Amen.[8]

Notes

1. Homer Clyde McEwen, Sr., "Conversations with a Gravedigger," *Preaching About Death*, ed. Alton M. Molter (Philadelphia: Fortress Press, 1975) 57–58.

2. Brian D. McLaren, *The Great Spiritual Migration* (New York: Convergent Books, 2016) 22.

3. A. W. W. Dale, *Life of R. W. Dale of Birmingham* (London: Hodder & Stoughton, 1898).

4. Eric Marshall and Stuart Hample, *Children's Letters to God* (New York: Workman Publishing, 1991).

5. Some books you might examine on this theme include the following: Eben Alexander, *Proof of Heaven*; Todd Burpo, *Heaven Is for Real*; Don Piper, *90 Minutes in Heaven*; and Raymond Moody, *Life after Life*. For a further treatment of the subject of death and life after death, examine my books, *Facing Grief and Death: Living with Dying* (Cleveland TN: Parson's Porch Books, 2013) and *The Journey to the Undiscovered Country: What's Beyond Death?* (Gonzalez FL: Energion Publications, 2012).

6. Eugene O'Neill, *Lazarus Laughed* (New York: Boni & Live Right, Inc., 1927).

7. McEwen, "Conversations with a Gravedigger," 59.

8. Joyce Rupp, *Prayer Seeds: A Gathering of Blessings, Reflections, and Poems for Spiritual Growth* (Notre Dame IN: Sorin Books, 2017) 77.

Other available titles from SMYTH & HELWYS

1, 2, 3 John and Jude (Annual Bible Study series)
Learning and Living the Truth
Judson Edwards

Studying these four letters will challenge readers to consider their own truth—the truth that governs their lives and the truth they feel is worth living and dying for. In a world where truth is a slippery reality, 1, 2, 3 John and Jude remind us that truth does exist and that truth still sets people free.
Teaching Guide 978-1-57312-982-4 152 pages/pb **$14.00**
Study Guide 978-1-57312-983-1 92 pages/pb **$6.00**

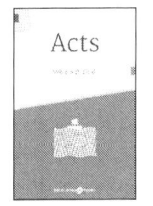

Acts (Preaching the Word Series)
William D. Shiell

In this collection of sermons on the book of Acts, William Shiell examines the disciples' efforts as they learned to share the gospel and foster character formation and fellowship. Shiell reveals how the resurrection of Jesus and the power of the Spirit disrupted cities across the Mediterranean—and how this message and Power are still capable of "turning the world upside down." 978-1-57312-906-0 234 pages/pb **$18.00**

Atonement in the Apocalypse
An Exposé of the Defeat of Evil
Robert W. Canoy

Revelation calls believers to see themselves through the unique lens of redemptive atonement and to live and model daily that they see themselves in the present moment as redeemed people. Having thus seen themselves, believers likewise are directed to see and to relate to others in this world the very way that God has seen them from eternity.
978-1-57312-946-6 218 pages/pb **$22.00**

Beginnings
A Reverend and a Rabbi Talk About the Stories of Genesis
Michael Smith and Rami Shapiro

Editor Aaron Herschel Shapiro declares that stories "must be retold—not just repeated, but reinvented, reimagined, and reexperienced" to remain vital in the world. Mike and Rami continue their conversations from the *Mount and Mountain* books, exploring the places where their traditions intersect and diverge, listening to each other as they respond to the stories of Genesis. 978-1-57312-772-1 202 pages/pb **$18.00**

To order call **1-800-747-3016** or visit **www.helwys.com**

Bugles in the Afternoon
Dealing with Discouragement and Disillusionment in Ministry
Judson Edwards

In *Bugles in the Afternoon*, Edwards writes, "My long experience in the church has convinced me that most ministers—both professional and lay—spend time under the juniper tree. Those ministers who have served more than ten years and not been depressed, discouraged, or disillusioned can hold their annual convention in a phone booth."

978-1-57312-865-0 148 pages/pb **$16.00**

A Christian's Guide to Islam
Michael D. McCullar

A Christian's Guide to Islam provides a brief but accurate guide to Muslim formation, history, structure, beliefs, practices, and goals. It explores to what degree the tenets of Islam have been misinterpreted, corrupted, or abused over the centuries.

978-1-57312-512-3 128 pages/pb **$16.00**

Countercultural Worship
A Plea to Evangelicals in a Secular Age
Mark G. McKim

Evangelical worship, McKim argues, has drifted far from both its biblical roots and historic origins, leaving evangelicals in danger of becoming mere chaplains to the wider culture, oblivious to the contradictions between what the secular culture says is real and important and what Scripture says is real and important.

978-1-57312-873-5 174 pages/pb **$19.00**

Crisis Ministry: A Handbook
Daniel G. Bagby

Covering more than 25 crisis pastoral care situations, this book provides a brief, practical guide for church leaders and other caregivers responding to stressful situations in the lives of parishioners. It tells how to resource caregiving professionals in the community who can help people in distress.

978-1-57312-370-9 154 pages/pb **$15.00**

Everyday Virtues
Classic Tales to Read with Kids
James A. Autry & Rick Autry

This book of stories collected by a father and grandfather team invites adults and children to read together. Featuring the six virtues of justice, humility, courage, compassion, freedom, and respect, these entertaining and easily understood stories from all over the world focus on what makes us truly human.

978-1-57312-971-8 220 pages/pb **$18.00**

To order call **1-800-747-3016** or visit **www.helwys.com**

Exemplars
Deacons as Servant and Spiritual Leaders
Elizabeth Allen and Daniel Vestal, eds.

Who Do Deacons Need to Be? What Do Deacons Need to Know? What Do Deacons Need to Do? These three questions form the basis for *Exemplars: Deacons as Servant and Spiritual Leaders*. They are designed to encourage robust conversation within diaconates as well as between deacons, clergy, and other laity. 978-1-57312-876-6 128 pages/pb **$15.00**

Faith, Hope & Politics
Inspiring a New Generation to Community-Changing Political Engagement
Brent McDougal

Through personal narrative, stories of inspiration, and a deep dive into fifteen qualities future leaders will need to make a lasting impact, Brent McDougal challenges the next generation to give their lives to a more hopeful and just future—a future in which faith, hope, and love have the power to transform America. 978-1-57312-992-3 174 pages/pb **$18.00**

Five Hundred Miles
Reflections on Calling and Pilgrimage
Lauren Brewer Bass

Spain's Camino de Santiago, the Way of St. James, has been a cherished pilgrimage path for centuries, visited by countless people searching for healing, solace, purpose, and hope. These stories from her five-hundred-mile-walk is Lauren Brewer Bass's honest look at the often winding, always surprising journey of a calling. 978-1-57312-812-4 142 pages/pb **$16.00**

A Five-Mile Walk
Exploring Themes in the Experience of Christian Faith and Discipleship
Michael B. Brown

Sometimes the Christian journey is a stroll along quiet shores. Other times it is an uphill climb on narrow, snow-covered mountain paths. Usually, it is simply walking in the direction of wholeness, one step after another, sometimes even two steps forward and one step back.
  978-1-57312-852-0 196 pages/pb **$18.00**

Glimpses from State Street
Wayne Ballard

As a collection of devotionals, *Glimpses from State Street* provides a wealth of insights and new ways to consider and develop our fellowship with Christ. It also serves as a window into the relationship between a small town pastor and a welcoming congregation.
  978-1-57312-841-4 156 pages/pb **$15.00**

To order call 1-800-747-3016 or visit www.helwys.com

God's Servants, the Prophets
Bryan Bibb

God's Servants, the Prophets covers the Israelite and Judean prophetic literature from the preexilic period. It includes Amos, Hosea, Isaiah, Micah, Zephaniah, Nahum, Habakkuk, Jeremiah, and Obadiah.

*978-1-57312-758-5 208 pages/pb **$16.00***

Holy Hilarity
A Funny Study of Genesis
Mark Roncace

Mark Roncace brings readers fifty-three short chapters of wit and amusing observations about the biblical stories, followed by five thought-provoking questions for individual reflection or group discussion. Humorous, yet reverent, this refreshing approach to Bible study invites us, whatever our background, to wrestle with the issues in the text and discover the ways those issues intersect our own messy lives. *978-157312-892-6 230 pages/pb **$17.00***

If Jesus Isn't the Answer . . . He Sure Asks the Right Questions!
J. Daniel Day

Taking eleven of Jesus' questions as its core, Day invites readers into their own conversation with Jesus. Equal parts testimony, theological instruction, pastoral counseling, and autobiography, the book is ultimately an invitation to honest Christian discipleship.

*978-1-57312-797-4 148 pages/pb **$16.00***

Judaism
A Brief Guide to Faith and Practice
Sharon Pace

Sharon Pace's newest book is a sensitive and comprehensive introduction to Judaism. How does belief in the One God and a universal morality shape the way in which Jews see the world? How does one find meaning in life and the courage to endure suffering? How does one mark joy and forge community ties? *978-1-57312-644-1 144 pages/pb **$16.00***

Live the Stories
50 Interactive Children's Sermons
Andrew Noe

Live the Stories provides church leaders a practical guide to teaching children during the worship service through play—and invites the rest of the congregation to join the fun. Noe's lessons allow children to play, laugh, and act out the stories of our faith and turn the sanctuary into a living testimony to what God has done in the past, is doing in the present, and will do in the future. *978-1-57312-943-5 128 pages/pb **$14.00***

To order call 1-800-747-3016 or visit www.helwys.com

The Lord's Prayer (Smyth & Helwys Bible Commentary Supplemental Series)
Nijay K. Gupta

The Lord's Prayer is the most recited, most memorized, and most studied text in the Bible. It also contains several conundrums: what does it mean to "hallow" the Father's name? What relationship does our forgiveness of others have with God's forgiveness for us? If God does not tempt, why would we pray "Lead us not into temptation"? This commentary not only addresses these important questions but also offers insight into how the global church throughout generations has interacted with the Lord's Prayer and has found in it inspiration and hope. 978-1-57312-984-8 200 pages/hc **$40.00**

Loyal Dissenters
Reading Scripture and Talking Freedom with 17th-century English Baptists
Lee Canipe

When Baptists in 17th-century England wanted to talk about freedom, they unfailingly began by reading the Bible—and what they found in Scripture inspired their compelling (and, ultimately, successful) arguments for religious liberty. In an age of widespread anxiety, suspicion, and hostility, these early Baptists refused to worship God in keeping with the king's command. 978-1-57312-872-8 178 pages/pb **$19.00**

Meditations on Luke
Daily Devotions from the Gentile Physician
Chris Cadenhead

Readers searching for a fresh encounter with Scripture can delve into *Meditations on Luke*, a collection of daily devotions intended to guide the reader through the book of Luke, which gives us some of the most memorable stories in all of Scripture. The Scripture, response, and prayer will guide readers' own meditations as they listen and respond to God's voice, coming to us through Luke's Gospel. 978-1-57312-947-3 328 pages/pb **$22.00**

A Pastoral Prophet
Sermons and Prayers of Wayne E. Oates
William Powell Tuck, ed.

Read these sermons and prayers and look directly into the heart of Wayne Oates. He was a consummate counselor, theologian, and writer, but first of all he was a pastor. . . . He gave voice to our deepest hurts, then followed with words we long to hear: you are not alone.

—Kay Shurden
Associate Professor Emeritus, Clinical Education,
Mercer University School of Medicine, Macon, Georgia
978-157312-955-8 160 pages/pb **$18.00**

To order call 1-800-747-3016 or visit www.helwys.com

Place Value
The Journey to Where You Are
Katie Sciba

Does a place have value? Can a place change us? Is it possible for God to use the place you are in to form you? From Victoria, Texas to Indonesia, Belize, Australia, and beyond, Katie Sciba's wanderlust serves as a framework to understand your own places of deep emotion and how God may have been weaving redemption around you all along.

978-157312-829-2 138 pages/pb **$15.00**

Portraits of Jesus
for an Age of Biblical Illiteracy
Gerald L. Borchert

Despite our era of communication and information overload, biblical illiteracy is widespread. In *Portraits of Jesus*, Gerald L. Borchert assists both ministers and laypeople with a return to what the New Testament writers say about this stunning Jesus who shocked the world and called a small company of believers into an electrifying transformation.

978-157312-940-4 212 pages/pb **$20.00**

Practicing Resurrection
Radical Hope in Difficult Times
Jeanie Miley

Through stories of her own literal and metaphorical journeys toward hope and renewal, Miley demonstrates that when we face hardship or the inevitable, difficult transitions in life, we may *practice resurrection*—and trust steadily in the goodness and mercy of God.

978-1-57312-972-5 218 pages/pb **$19.00**

Preaching that Connects
Charles B. Bugg and Alan Redditt

How does the minister stay focused on the holy when the daily demands of the church seem relentless? How do we come to a preaching event with a sense that God is working in us and through us? In *Preaching that Connects*, Charles Bugg and Alan Redditt explore the balancing act of a minister's authority as preacher, sharing what the congregation needs to hear, and the communal role as pastor, listening to God alongside congregants.

978-157312-887-2 128 pages/pb **$15.00**

To order call 1-800-747-3016 or visit www.helwys.com

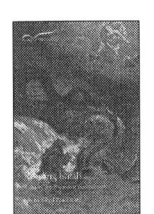

Reading Isaiah
(Reading the Old Testament series)
A Literary and Theological Commentary

Hyun Chul Paul Kim

While closely exegeting key issues of each chapter, this commentary also explores interpretive relevance and significance between ancient texts and the modern world. Engaging with theological messages of the book of Isaiah as a unified whole, the commentary will both illuminate and inspire readers to wrestle with its theological implications for today's church and society.

978-1-57312-925-1 352 pages/pb **$33.00**

Reading Jeremiah
(Reading the Old Testament series)
A Literary and Theological Commentary

Corrine Carvalho

Reflecting the ways that communal tragedy permeates communal identity, the book of Jeremiah as literary text embodies the confusion, disorientation, and search for meaning that all such tragedy elicits. Just as the fall of Jerusalem fractured the Judean community and undercut every foundation on which it built its identity, so too the book itself (or more properly, the scroll) jumbles images, genres, and perspectives.

978-1-57312-924-4 186 pages/pb **$32.00**

Ruth & Esther (Smyth & Helwys Bible Commentary)

Kandy Queen-Sutherland

Ruth and Esther are the only two women for whom books of the Hebrew Bible are named. This distinction in itself sets the books apart from other biblical texts that bear male names, address the community through its male members, recall the workings of God and human history through a predominately male perspective, and look to the future through male heirs. These books are particularly stories of survival. The story of Ruth focuses on the survival of a family; Esther focuses on the survival of a people.

978-1-57312-891-9 544 pages/hc **$60.00**

Seeing in the Dark
Biblical Meditations for People Dealing with Depression

Ronald D. Vaughan

This collection of biblical meditations is designed to be used as a daily devotional resource. Along with each meditation is a prayer based on that chapter's life lesson and a truth to affirm, a short summary to help readers remember what they've learned.

978-1-57312-973-2 144 pages/pb **$18.00**

To order call **1-800-747-3016** or visit **www.helwys.com**

Seeing the Son on the Way to the Moon
A NASA Engineer's Reflection on Science and Faith
W. Merlin Merritt

W. Merlin Merritt recounts his experiences during the early NASA space program and describes his struggle to integrate faith and science. He ultimately concludes that technology can point us to the grandeur of God's universe. The immensity and wonders of the cosmos point not only to an intelligent creator God but also to One who is actively involved in the universe.
978-1-57312-942-8 130 pages/pb **$14.00**

Sessions with Isaiah (Sessions Bible Studies series)
What to Do When the World Caves In
James M. King

The book of Isaiah begins in the years of national stress when, under various kings, Israel was surrounded by more powerful neighbors and foolishly sought foreign alliances rather than dependence on Yahweh. It continues with the natural result of that unfaithfulness: conquest by the great power in the region, Babylon, and the captivity of many of Israel's best and brightest in that foreign land. The book concludes anticipating their return to the land of promise and strong admonitions about the people's conduct—but we also hear God's reassuring messages of comfort and restoration, offered to all who repent.
978-1-57312-942-8 130 pages/pb **$14.00**

Stained-Glass Millennials
Rob Lee

We've heard the narrative that millennials are done with the institutional church; they've packed up and left. This book is an alternative to that story and chronicles the journey of millennials who are investing their lives in the institution because they believe in the church's resurrecting power. Through anecdotes and interviews, Rob Lee takes readers on a journey toward God's unfolding future for the church, a beloved institution in desperate need of change.
978-1-57312-926-8 156 pages/pb **$16.00**

Star Thrower
A Pastor's Handbook
William Powell Tuck

In *Star Thrower: A Pastor's Handbook*, William Powell Tuck draws on over fifty years of experience to share his perspective on being an effective pastor. He describes techniques for sermon preparation, pastoral care, and church administration, as well as for conducting Communion, funeral, wedding, and baptismal services. He also includes advice for working with laity and church staff, coping with church conflict, and nurturing one's own spiritual and family life.
978-1-57312-889-6 244 pages/pb **$15.00**

To order call **1-800-747-3016** or visit **www.helwys.com**

Tell the Truth, Shame the Devil
Stories about the Challenges of Young Pastors
James Elllis III, ed.

A pastor's life is uniquely difficult. *Tell the Truth, Shame the Devil*, then, is an attempt to expose some of the challenges that young clergy often face. While not exhaustive, this collection of essays is a superbly compelling and diverse introduction to how tough being a pastor under the age of thirty-five can be.　　　978-1-57312-839-1　198 pages/pb　**$18.00**

Though the Darkness Gather Round
Devotions about Infertility, Miscarriage, and Infant Loss
Mary Elizabeth Hill Hanchey and Erin McClain, eds.

Much courage is required to weather the long grief of infertility and the sudden grief of miscarriage and infant loss. This collection of devotions by men and women, ministers, chaplains, and lay leaders who can speak of such sorrow, is a much-needed resource and precious gift for families on this journey and the faith communities that walk beside them.

978-1-57312-811-7　180 pages/pb　**$19.00**

Time for Supper
Invitations to Christ's Table
Brett Younger

Some scholars suggest that every meal in literature is a communion scene. Could every meal in the Bible be a communion text? Could every passage be an invitation to God's grace? These meditations on the Lord's Supper help us listen to the myriad of ways God invites us to gratefully, reverently, and joyfully share the cup of Christ.　　978-1-57312-720-2　246 pages/pb　**$18.00**

A True Hope
Jedi Perils and the Way of Jesus
Joshua Hays

Star Wars offers an accessible starting point for considering substantive issues of faith, philosophy, and ethics. In *A True Hope*, Joshua Hays explores some of these challenging ideas through the sayings of the Jedi Masters, examining the ways the worldview of the Jedi is at odds with that of the Bible.　　　978-1-57312-770-7　186 pages/pb　**$18.00**

To order call 1-800-747-3016 or visit www.helwys.com

Clarence Jordan's
Cotton Patch Gospel

The Complete Collection

The Cotton Patch Gospel, by Koinonia Farm founder Clarence Jordan, recasts the stories of Jesus and the letters of the New Testament into the language and culture of the mid-twentieth-century South. Born out of the civil rights struggle, these now-classic translations of much of the New Testament bring the far-away places of Scripture closer to home: Gainesville, Selma, Birmingham, Atlanta, Washington D.C.

Hardback
448 pages
Regular Price $50.00
Online Price $25.00

Paperback
448 pages
Regular Price $40.00
Online Price $20.00

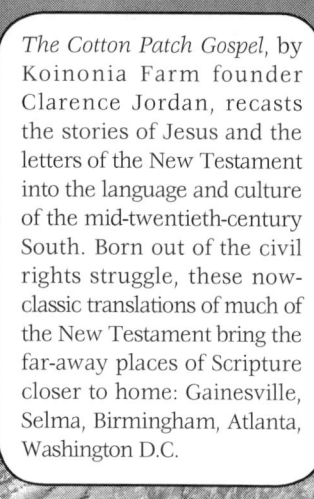

More than a translation, *The Cotton Patch Gospel* continues to make clear the startling relevance of Scripture for today. Now for the first time collected in a single, hardcover volume, this edition comes complete with a new Introduction by President Jimmy Carter, a Foreword by Will D. Campbell, and an Afterword by Tony Campolo. Smyth & Helwys Publishing is proud to help reintroduce these seminal works of Clarence Jordan to a new generation of believers, in an edition that can be passed down to generations still to come.

SMYTH & HELWYS
To order call **1-800-747-3016**
or visit **www.helwys.com**

Made in the USA
Middletown, DE
21 December 2018